GREAT BRIDGES

From Ancient Times to the Twentieth Century

WILBUR J. WATSON

WITH TWO HUNDRED ILLUSTRATIONS

DOVER PUBLICATIONS, INC.
MINEOLA, NEW YORK

Bibliographical Note

This Dover edition, first published in 2006, is an unabridged republication of the work originally published in 1927 by William Helburn, Inc., New York, under the title *Bridge Architecture, Containing Two-Hundred Illustrations of the Notable Bridges of the World, Ancient and Modern with Descriptive, Historical and Legendary Text.*

Library of Congress Cataloging-in-Publication Data

Watson, Wilbur J. (Wilbur Jay), 1871–1939.
    [Bridge architecture]
    Great bridges : from ancient times to the twentieth century / Wilbur J. Watson.
      p. cm.
    Reprint. Originally published under title: Bridge architecture. New York, W. Helburn, c1927.
    Includes bibliographical references and index.
    ISBN 0-486-44743-X (pbk.)
    1. Bridges. I. Title.

TG15.W3 2006
624.2—dc22

                      2006040322

Manufactured in the United States of America
Dover Publications, Inc., 31 East 2nd Street, Mineola, N.Y. 11501

Affectionately dedicated
to
CADY STALEY, Ph.D., LL.D.
President Emeritus of Case School of Applied Science
Cleveland, Ohio

I like a bridge—
It cries, "Come on
"I'll take you there from here and
            here from there
"And save you time and toil."

I like a bridge—
It breathes romance;
"There's new adventure on the
            further side
"And I will help you cross."

I like a bridge—
It makes me think
That when a worry comes, my
            mind will find
Somewhere a friendly bridge.

                    —*W. G. R.*

"Bridges ought to have the self-same qualifications we judge necessary in all other buildings, which are that they should be commodious, beautiful and lasting."
—*Andrea Palladio, 1518-1580*

"In the history of Architecture, those bridges are the most attractive which are something more than mere passages for carriages and pedestrians."
—*Russell Sturgis*

LIST OF ILLUSTRATIONS

ILLUSTRATIONS

ILLUSTRATIONS

ILLUSTRATIONS

ILLUSTRATIONS

ILLUSTRATIONS

ILLUSTRATIONS

SEGOVIA, SPAIN—DETAIL OF ROMAN AQUEDUCT—98 A.D.

PHOTO BY LOUIS LA BEAUME

GREAT BRIDGES

THE late Daniel H. Burnham once defined architecture as "the art of creating an agreeable form." Bridge architecture then may be defined as the art of creating bridges agreeable in form; an art, of course, that must conform to the requirements of the science of bridge engineering.

Granting that human happiness is greatly enhanced by beautiful and pleasing surroundings, it is highly desirable that utilitarian structures such as bridges should be as pleasing to the eye as it is practicable to make them and that there should be greater collaboration between the architect and the engineer with a realization on the part of each that science without art is apt to be unattractive and art without science inefficient.

The purpose of this work is to illustrate the art of good bridge design, both as to composition and detail, as exemplified by ancient and modern bridges, utilizing selected photographs for this purpose.

The text includes descriptions of many of the bridges illustrated, some historical data and considerable literary and legendary lore, all of which the author hopes will be found of interest to the lay reader, as well as to the engineer and the architect. With this object in view, technical terms have been avoided as much as possible and technical data for the most part has been omitted.

The data contained herein has been gathered from many sources, but largely from the books listed under "Bibliography." The photographs have been collected over a period of years from many sources. Wherever possible, full credit has been given to the designers of the structure illustrated, and also to the source from which the photograph was obtained.

The reader will note that many of the best designed bridges of the Modern Period are those in the design of which engineers and architects collaborated.

Critical quotations from various writers, ancient and modern, have been freely used in this text, and the reader will note that there is considerable disagreement among these writers on many questions of architectural design, such as the propriety of using the classical architectural motives as ornamental features on bridges.

While a small amount of original criticism of certain designs and tendencies will be found in the text, it has been the author's aim to bring together, under a single cover, a considerable number of illustrations of selected designs for critical study by the reader.

The bridge is one of the most important of architectural developments, and it is with the hope of quickening interest in the subject that this volume has been prepared.

Special acknowledgment for valuable assistance is made to Professor F. H. Neff, Professor F. H. Constant, Professor Geo. S. Beggs, Mr. Clement E. Chase, all members of the American Society of Civil Engineers, to Mr. A. T. North, member of the American Institute of Architects, and to Mr. William Ganson Rose, editorial counsellor.

GREAT BRIDGES

BRIDGES ARE CONSIDERED HEREIN AS DIVIDED INTO FIVE TYPES, EACH
TYPE UTILIZING A DIFFERENT MECHANICAL PRINCIPLE
AS THE BASIS OF ITS DESIGN, AS FOLLOWS:

THE ARCH

The Arch, the mechanical principle of which is that of a
curved structure, the elements depending upon the com-
pressive strength of the material used. The corresponding
example in nature is the natural stone arch.

THE SIMPLE BEAM

The Simple Beam, depending primarily upon the bending
strength of the material. The natural example is that of
the fallen tree spanning a stream.

THE SUSPENSION

The Suspension, or cable bridge, utilizing the simple principle of the cord in direct tension, as illustrated in nature
by the swinging vine, utilized by monkeys in passing from
one tree to another.

THE CANTILEVER

The Cantilever, making use of mechanical principles similar to those of the simple beam, but requiring an anchorage at one end. Quite probably, primitive man discovered the principle at a very early stage of his development, and made use of it to construct longer spans than he was able to build with simple beams.

THE TRUSS

The Truss, requiring the use of connected members, some in compression, some in tension, and some as simple beams, seems to have been utterly beyond the comprehension of the barbarian, and, in fact, belongs almost exclusively to modern civilization.

CLASSIFICATION BY PERIODS

HISTORICALLY, bridges are conveniently assigned to six periods:

FIRST PERIOD

The Ancient Period, preceding the Roman Era, during which most bridges, in Europe, at least, were of the beam type. Arch bridges were probably built in China prior to the Roman Era, and the arch was used by the ancient Egyptians in other constructions.

SECOND PERIOD

The Roman Period, during which the Romans introduced the extensive use of the arch principle, dating from 300 B. C. to 300 A. D., covering a period of about 600 years.

THIRD PERIOD

The Middle Ages in Europe, from the eleventh to the sixteenth centuries, characterized chiefly by the construction of massive, more or less crudely designed and executed arches of masonry, but including also many arches of bold and slender proportions. During this period, practically all culture was centered in the religious orders, and, therefore, most of the bridges were built by monks. During this period finer work was probably being done by the Chinese.

FOURTH PERIOD

The Renaissance in Europe, occurring during the sixteenth and seventeenth centuries, exhibited much greater refinement of both design and construction. It is worthy of note that up to the eighteenth century, no distinction was made between the architect and the engineer, the master builders of those days devoting their talents to the design of both buildings and bridges.

FIFTH PERIOD

The Eighteenth Century, including the first quarter of the nineteenth, during which the masonry arch reached its greatest perfection, and engineers, skilled and specializing in bridge construction, made their appearance. Prominent among these first bridge engineers were the Rennies in England and Perronet in France.

SIXTH PERIOD

The Modern Period, beginning with the advent of the railroad about 1830, and characterized by the utilization of all of the five basic types, but more especially by the perfection of the truss type, due to the availability of structural iron and steel.

PLATE I—UTAH—THE EDWIN NATURAL BRIDGE

PHOTO FROM TIMES WIDE WORLD PHOTOS, NEW YORK

PLATE II—BHUTAN, ASIA—PRIMITIVE TIMBER CANTILEVER BRIDGE—130-FOOT SPAN

PHOTO BY JOHN CLAUDE WHITE, LONDON

PLATE III—CHUNG-KING, CHINA—COVERED MASONRY ARCH—AGE UNKNOWN
PHOTO FROM WORLD SERVICE AGENCIES OF THE METHODIST EPISCOPAL CHURCH

PLATE IV—PU'TO'SHAN, CHINA—BRIDGE TO THE MONASTERY OF THE RAIN OF LAW, SACRED ISLAND OF PU'LO'

PHOTO FROM "PICTURESQUE CHINA," BY ERNST BOERSCHMANN

PLATE V—HANCHOU, CHINA—STONE SLAB BRIDGE

FROM "PICTURESQUE CHINA," ERNST BOERSCHMANN

PLATE VI—CASHMERE, ASIA—TIMBER ARCH BRIDGE OVER THE JHELAM RIVER AT SRINAGAR

COPYRIGHT BY PUBLISHERS PHOTO SERVICE, NEW YORK

PLATE VII—CHINA—SUSPENSION BRIDGE AT SZE-CHUAN

PHOTO BY ROBT. F. FITCH

PLATE VIII—CONSTANTINOPLE—BRIDGE OVER THE GOLDEN HORN—PONTOON TYPE

PHOTO FROM MASCHINENFABRIK AUGSBURG-NÜRNBERG A. G.

I. THE ANCIENT PERIOD

Ancient Cantilever Bridges in Asia

BRIDGES of this type are common today in Central Asia, and have been in existence since ancient times. The timber parts, of course, require periodic replacement, but the design has probably remained unchanged for ages.

Plate II shows a bridge in Bhutan, which is of unknown age, but reputed to be very old. The span of this particular bridge is 130 feet. The photograph was taken by John Claude White.

Ancient Chinese Arches

Many fine stone arches are to be found in China; and while little definite data is available regarding them, and especially their ages, enough is known to prove that many of them are perhaps over 2000 years old, although some of those herein illustrated are probably of comparatively recent date, but may be considered as representative of an art that is, in itself, undoubtedly ancient. Some of these structures are beautiful and demonstrate that the Chinese were familiar with many refinements of the art long before these refinements were practiced in Europe. For instance, the projecting extradosal course, which appears first in European bridge architecture about the fifteenth century, was used in an old structure at Chung-King, shown in Plate III.

Has Europe anything that surpasses the simple beauty of the structure at Pu'to'shan, photographed by Ernst Boerschmann and illustrated in his "Picturesque China"? (Plate IV.)

Some of these old Chinese masonry bridges are quite long. Boerschmann shows one comprising fourteen arches, and similar bridges are described in the writings of Marco Polo, who visited China in the thirteenth century A. D. The Chinese have also some interesting bridges of other types than the arch. For instance, there is a bridge of stone slabs on stone piers at Hanchou, the piers decorated with carved heads of animals. (Plate V, Boerschmann.)

There also exist in Eastern Asia good examples of bridges of the timber arch type supported on stone piers, as shown by a bridge in Cashmere, Plate VI, and the suspension type, illustrated by a bridge in Northern Sze-Chuan, built of bamboo cables about eight inches in diameter, Plate VII. In Japan there are many beautiful bridges of timber, most of them utilizing the beam principle, and renewed as required. The rebuilt structure is usually an exact reproduction of the old, thus perpetuating the design, which may be ancient, while the existing structure is recent.

Little is known regarding the ancient bridges of Western Asia. It is supposed that brick arch bridges spanned the Euphrates at Babylon, and a writer asserts that one of these had a span of 660 feet, a statement that seems improbable, and not to be taken seriously.

Some early writers and travelers must have possessed vivid imaginations. George Semple, writing in 1776, describes a stone bridge in China, which he calls the Bridge over the River Saffrany, spanning 600 feet in a single arch, and having a height from its foundation to the top of the parapets of 750 feet and which was known to travelers as the Flying Bridge. It must have flown away.

There are old bridges in Persia, but definite information regarding them is not obtainable. Some were undoubtedly Roman in origin. One at Dizful, over the river Diz, has a length of 1250 feet, contains twenty pointed arches, and is variously dated from 350 B.C. to 300 A.D. Many of these old Persian bridges are built of brick and reflect the influence of Byzantine architecture.

Ancient Pontoon or Floating Bridges

Herodotus tells us that Xerxes built a pontoon bridge over the Hellespont to facilitate his invasion of Greece in the year 480 B.C. According to the noted historian, this bridge was double, consisting of one line of 360 boats and another of 314, the construction being quite similar to the military pontoon bridges of the present day, extensively used in the World War.

Herodotus states that it took the Persians seven days and nights to pass over it, marching in two steady streams. The width of the straits at this point is about a mile, which would correspond to a spacing of the boats of about fifteen feet. Similar bridges are mentioned by Homer, who lived in the ninth century B.C., and Xenophon describes one he built over the Tigris in the "Retreat of the Ten Thousand."

These pontoon bridges belong to the beam type, the stationary piers being replaced by boats or pontoons, which support the ends of the beams that carry the roadway platform. They are crude, requiring but little architectural skill.

While the pontoon type is usually employed for temporary purposes only, some existing structures have served for very long periods, with more or less frequent repairs and rebuilding. One of the most important of such bridges is that over the Golden Horn at Constantinople, recently rebuilt, and illustrated by Plate VIII.

Ancient Pile or Trestle Bridges

The Sublician is supposed to have been the first bridge over the River Tiber constructed by the Romans, and was famous as the bridge defended so heroically by Horatius Cocles, who single-handed held the Etruscan army at bay while his comrades destroyed the bridge behind him. As a matter of fact, it was a crude pile and beam structure of timber, the precise details of the construction being a matter of conjecture. Such timber pile bridges are doubtless of ancient origin, as the pre-historic lake dwellers of Europe used a similar construction on which to build their rude huts, which were accessible only by means of a pile and beam bridge connecting with the land, the ancient prototype of the modern timber trestle so familiar to us all.

At one time, about 620 B.C., the Sublician Bridge was rebuilt by the Chief Priests, to whom its maintenance seems to have been entrusted. It is said that they thereupon assumed the title of pontifices, a title which was appropriated and perpetuated by the Christian Church and is supposed to be the origin of the title of the Popes, The Holy Pontiffs.

According to the Encyclopedia Britannica, the word "pontifex" is evidently derived from "pons" (bridge), and "facere," and is believed to have a connection of some kind with the sacred bridge over the Tiber known as the Pons Sublicius, although this is disputed. The Collegium of the Pontifices was the most important priesthood of Rome. The head of the order came to be known, under the Republic, as the Pontifex Maximus, and under the Empire this title was assumed by the Emperors themselves. With the decay of the Empire and rise of the Christian Church to temporal power, this title naturally fell to the Popes. So the highest religious title in Christendom probably is derived from, or is synonymic with, that of the humble bridge builder.

The Pons Sublicius seems never to have been rebuilt in stone, but was always retained as a timber bridge, possibly for sentimental reasons.

Caesar's Bridge over the Rhine

The military bridge which Julius Caesar said he built across the Rhine in ten days' time has been a model for timber pile bridges ever since. The design consisted of pile piers which were protected by ice breakers formed of groups of three piles. These pile piers were capped with rough timbers which supported the lintels or beams, also of rough timbers,

and these in turn carried the flooring, a description easily recognized as applying to the typical modern timber trestle bridge. This bridge was about 12¼ meters (40 feet) wide and 425 to 525 meters (1300 to 1600 feet) in length. The individual spans were approximately 6½ to 8 meters (20 to 25 feet).

The work is thus described in Caesar's Commentaries, the dimensions being given in Roman feet, only slightly different from the modern unit of the same name.

"He joined together at the distance of two feet, two piles each a foot and a half thick, sharpened a little at the lower end, and proportioned in length to the depth of the river. After he had, by means of engines (pile driver or any other machinery), sunk these into the river and fixed them at the bottom, and then driven them in with rammers, not quite perpendicularly like a stake, but bending forward and sloping, so as to incline in the direction of the current of the river; he also placed two other piles opposite to these, at the distance of forty feet lower down, fastened together in the same manner but directed against the force and current of the river. Both these, moreover, were kept firmly apart by beams two feet thick (the space which the binding of the piles occupied), laid in at their extremities between two braces on each side; and in consequence of these being in different directions and fastened on sides the one opposite to the other, so great was the strength of the work, and such the arrangement of the materials, that in proportion as the greater body of water dashed against the bridge, so much the closer were its parts held fastened together. These beams were bound together by timber laid over them in the direction of the length of the bridge and were then covered over with laths and hurdles; and in addition to this, piles were driven into the water obliquely, at the lower side of the bridge, and these serving as buttresses, and being connected with every portion of the work, sustained the force of the stream; and there were others also above the bridge at a moderate distance; that if trunks of trees or vessels were floated down the river by the barbarians for the purpose of destroying the work, the violence of such things might be diminished by these defences, and might not injure the bridge. Within ten days after the timber began to be collected the whole work was completed, and the whole army led over."

Like most military bridges, this famous structure was short lived, being cut down by order of Caesar himself only eighteen days later, having served its purpose. Without doubt, the Roman armies built many such structures.

The pile or trestle bridge, like the pontoon type, admits of but slight architectural treatment, although many such structures have

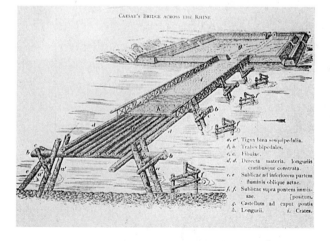

been embellished with more or less artistic timber railings, and, when of rustic design, used for small and light bridges, can be made very attractive.

Trajan's Bridge over the Danube

This was one of the most famous of the early Roman Bridges, and while neither an accurate description nor sufficient ruins for reconstructing it have come down to us, it is known to have consisted of twenty spans of timber arches, supported upon masonry piers, and was therefore the first notable example of the use of this combination. The ruins of thirteen piers are still visible at the site, which is just above the "Iron Gate" of the Danube.

The design is illustrated on the Arch of Trajan at Rome, and attributed to one Apollodorus of Damascus.

This bridge was built by Trajan in order that he might the more readily get at the barbarians to the north of the Danube, and it is of interest, historically, to note that a little later it was demolished by order of the Emperor Hadrian because, it is said, the tables had been turned and the barbarians were using it in order to get back at the Romans. Ancient records state that this project was completed in a single season.

These timber bridges constructed by the Romans were only copies of types that doubtless were common in Europe as well as in Asia for many centuries preceding the Roman era and they therefore belong, historically, to ancient times.

The true Roman Era in bridge building began with the use of the masonry arch, which the Romans developed to a high degree of perfection. Nevertheless, the typical Roman bridge was doubtless always a timber pile trestle, even in the days of the Empire, and, that these structures were not always well built or safe is shown by many references to them in Roman literature, such as the following human quotation from Catullus:

"O, Colonia, you who desire to sport on a long bridge and are prepared to hold your feasts, but you fear the shaky legs of the little bridge standing on second hand sticks, lest it would tumble flat, and lie in the deep marsh. O, Colonia, give me this gift, of a great laugh, if a good bridge on which the sacred feasts of the Saturnalia might be held is given to you for your games. I wish that a certain fellow townsman of mine might fall from your bridge head over heels into the mud and in truth where the lake and the brimy, stinking swamp is darkest and deepest." Catullus (87-55 B. C.)

It seems strange that the Greeks, who developed an architecture so beautiful and perfect that it has remained the wonder of all succeeding ages, built no bridges worthy of mention. The answer is to be found in the fact that the Greeks built no great highways; they were a sea-faring people and their one great highway was the Mediterranean Sea, on the shores of which they founded their beautiful cities, and over the waters of which they maintained intercity communication.

II. THE ROMAN PERIOD

Roman Bridges over the Tiber at Rome
There are in existence today, wholly or partially intact, six old bridges over the Tiber dating back to Roman times, the Ponte Rotto, the Ponte Sisto, the Ponte Quattro Capi, the Ponte St. Angelo, the Ponte Molle and the Ponte Cestius.

The Ponte Rotto, known to the Romans as the Pons Aemilius (named for the Pontifex Maximus M. Aemilius Lepidus) and to Palladio as the Pons Palatinus, is the most ancient of existing Roman Bridges, but the present ruins of the arches are believed, in the absence of historical records, to be replacements, at least in part, of the original spans. The arches have spans of 24 meters* and the material used was peperino and tufa for the arches, with a facing of travertine. These same materials were used for the other existing Roman bridges. (Plate IX.)

The Ponte Sisto as it now exists is believed to have been rebuilt upon the foundations of the old Pons Aurelius or Palatine Bridge by Pope Sixtus IV about 1480, so that probably only parts are Roman. (Plate X.)

The present Ponte Quattro Capi is the ancient Bridge of Fabricius, built in the year 62 B. C. and is practically intact as then built. The modern name is derived from an emblem representing the four-headed Janus, carved on the bridge parapet. The arches have spans of 25 and 34 meters and the width is 15 meters. The structure was repaired in 1680.

The two segmental arches spring from the water level and the spandrel over the center pier is pierced by a large arched opening flanked by two pilasters carried to the cop-

*One meter equals 3.28 feet.

ing line. There is a pleasing contrast between the large stones of the arch rings and parapet and the small material used for the spandrel walls. (Plate XI.)

The Ponte St. Angelo is the Pons Aelius of Roman times, built by the Emperor Hadrian in 134 A. D., and consisted of eight arches having a maximum span of 20 meters. The present parapets were added in the seventeenth century and contain ten statues by Bernini, the architect who designed the great Colonnade of St. Peter's. The modern bridge has but five arches admitted to be part of the original construction. These arches have projecting extradosal courses and carefully coursed masonry throughout. (Plate XII.)

The Pons Milvius (modern Ponte Molle), located on the Flaminian Way, was built originally in 109 B. C., by M. Aemilius Scaurus, but only parts of the present structure are believed to be the original work. (Plate XIII.)

The Pons Cestius (modern Ponte St. Bartolomew), built in 43 B. C. and rebuilt about 370 A. D., is in good condition and contains much of the original masonry in spite of numerous restorations. It consists of a single arch.

Roman Bridge at Rimini, Italy

This is a fine example of Roman bridge building and is also noted as being the oldest known bridge built on a skew (with the piers not at right angles with the axis of the bridge). The amount of skew is only 13 degrees and the arch rings are built with horizontal joints. The spans are five in number, from 8½ to 11 meters in length, supported by piers about 6½ meters thick.

The material used for the facing is marble and the spandrels are decorated with niches, flanked by pilasters carrying an entablature and pediment. Dentils are also used under the overhanging parapet or coping course. The architectural embellishment is unusual for a Roman bridge, most of them being extremely plain and entirely devoid of applied ornament. This structure was built by the Emperor Augustus in 14 A. D., and is known as the Ponte di Augusto. (Plate XIV.)

The Pont du Gard, Nimes

The Romans required large quantities of water for use in their baths and amphitheatres and as they did not possess the necessary materials to build pipes to resist large internal pressures, they could not use the siphon principle upon which modern engineers rely, and were, therefore, compelled to build numerous huge aqueducts to bring the water to them by gravity. There are many remains of these aqueducts at Rome and in the provinces. One of the best preserved examples is the aqueduct at Nimes in France, attributed to the Emperor Agrippa and to the year 14 A.D., although this is uncertain. The total length of the conduit is 40 kilometers, the aqueduct bridge itself being about 262 meters long and 51.7 meters high.

The design consists of three tiers of arches, the effect of mass being augmented by the projection of numerous stones from the faces of piers and spandrels. These projecting stones were used for the support of scaffolding during construction.

"The stone of this bridge is a yellowish

color. Seen under the sun from the west side, the bridge has a brightish yellow tint, with patches of dark color, due to the weather. The stone in the highest tier is a concretion of shells and sand, and that in the lower tiers appears to be the same. The stones of the two lower layers are without cement; but the arches of the upper tier, which are built with much smaller stones, are cemented." (Sir William Smith.) The conduit itself is of concrete, 1.30 meters wide and 1.60 meters high (Sparrow) and the thickness of the bed is 22 centimeters. The arches of the lower tier have spans of 26.4 meters each. A roadway has been added to the structure at the level of the first tier of arches. This is a modern addition. (Plate XV.)

".... It bridges the streams and it strides o'er the plain;

TOWER AT CENTER OF ALCANTARA BRIDGE

In its arm is the river it sets down again
For the fevered metropolis' dower."

(Song of the Roman Arch—Durward.)

There exist throughout France many fine examples of Roman Bridges. Worthy of especial note is the bridge at Sommieres, consisting of seventeen semi-circular arches, and still in use, and a small but exquisite structure near St. Chamas, known as the Pont Flavien, comprising elaborate arched memorial portals at each end. The name is taken from an inscription on the arch portals which records that one Donnius Flavius, a priest from the temple of Rome and Augustus, ordered its erection in his will. (Plate XVI.)

Bridge at Alcantara, Spain, over the Tagus, on the Via Lata (Puente Trajan a' Alcantara)

This bridge is one of the most famous as well as one of the best preserved of Roman Bridges and is attributed to the Emperor Trajan, himself a native of Spain, at approximately 98 A. D.

The central span is 30 meters long and the height above the river is about 30 meters. There are six spans in all, making a length of bridge of 188 meters, and carrying a roadway 8 meters wide, an unusual width for a Roman Bridge. The architect was Caius Julius Lacer, whose name is contained in an inscription on the bridge, and the funds were raised in the Roman province of Lusitania, in which the bridge was located.

This noble monument to Roman enterprise and skill was partly destroyed in the thirteenth century and restored in the fifteenth, and again partly destroyed in the early part of the nineteenth century and fully restored about 1860. Al Kan'tara means in Arabian "The Bridge." (Plate XVII.)

Roman Aqueduct at Segovia, Spain

This is one of the best preserved, as well as one of the noblest, of Roman Aqueducts. It also was built by the Emperor Trajan, about the same time as the bridge at Alcantara, 98 A. D., and is also constructed of granite blocks, laid without mortar. This structure is built with offsets at the tops of the several tiers, obtaining the effect of battered walls, by decreasing the thickness of the several stages—a detail of design essentially Roman.

There are 119 arches, in two tiers, and the length is 876 meters for the arch structure, flanked by a solid wall 880 meters long. This structure is known locally as the Devil's Bridge, one of the many so-called, and the name is connected with a legend, which is charmingly told in "Castilian Days" by John Hay. "The Evil One was in love with a pretty girl of the upper town and full of protestations of love. The fair Segovian listened to him one evening, when her plump arms ached with the work of bringing water from the Ravina, and promised eyes to favor if his Infernal Majesty would build an aqueduct to her door before morning. He worked all night, like the devil, and the maiden, opening her black eyes at sunrise, saw him putting the last stone in the last arch, as the first ray of the sun lighted on his shining tail. The Church, we think very unfairly, decided that he had failed, and released the coquettish contractor from her promise, and it is said

that the devil has never trusted a Segovian out of his sight since."

Study of the detail photographs of this structure, taken by Louis La Beaume, show plainly the Roman methods of construction. All stones have at least one exposed face and the bonds are quite regular, with an occasional header extending clear across the arch soffit, which is quite narrow. (Plates XVIII, XIX, & XX.)

Roman Engineering

The bridges built by the Romans were merely links in a great, comprehensive system of highly improved highways connecting all parts of the great Roman Empire with the Eternal City. The expression "All roads lead to Rome" was a verity.

It has been said that a resident of Britain in Roman times—and the Romans lived in Britain for nearly four hundred years—could drive to London, embark there for the mainland, and after crossing the channel could drive to Rome over highly improved and paved roads without fording a single stream.

The roads were one of the great outstanding achievements of the Roman genius. Their art they borrowed, or rather commandeered, from the Greeks, but their engineering was the expression of their own spirit.

Roman engineering skill was not confined to the construction of roads and bridges, however, but included magnificent buildings, great baths and the aqueducts and sewers to serve them, amphitheaters that have never been excelled, and, of course, military defences of all kinds.

Only a few of the vast number of Roman

bridges have survived the ravages of time, of war and of flood; most have perished, but those few are marvels of engineering skill. The Romans, however, did not, as a rule, exercise as much care in the construction of foundations for their structures as they did for the superstructures. A common method of founding in water was to divert the stream temporarily, or build open cofferdams to exclude the water, and when this was not practicable, loose stones were often thrown into the water until a platform was obtained, of sufficient size to serve as a foundation for the coursed masonry.

The Romans understood and practised pile-driving, an art very much more ancient than Roman History, and they are known to have used timber centering for their arches, quite similar to that used today.

The labor employed in the construction of these great Roman bridges was doubtless mostly slave labor, and the workmen used tools and machines of the simplest sort, the wedge, the lever, the windlass.

PLATE IX—ROME—PONTE ROTTO—ROMAN PERIOD
FROM AN ETCHING BY ROSSINI. *1822*

PLATE X—ROME—PONTE SISTO. PARTLY ROMAN. RESTORED IN FIFTEENTH CENTURY

PHOTO FROM RAU STUDIOS. PHILADELPHIA

PLATE XI—ROME—PONTE QUATTRO CAPI—62 B.C. AND LATER RESTORATIONS

PHOTO BY ANDERSON

PLATE XII—ROME—PONTE S. ANGELO—HADRIAN, 134 A.D.—PARAPETS ADDED IN SEVENTEENTH CENTURY

PHOTO FROM THE DETROIT PUBLISHING CO.

PLATE XIII—ROME—PONTE MOLLE—ROMAN PERIOD, 109 B.C. AND RESTORATIONS

PHOTO BY ED. BROGI

PLATE XIV—RIMINI, ITALY—PONTE DI AUGUSTO—ROMAN, A.D. 14

PHOTO FROM ED. BROGI

PLATE XV—NIMES, FRANCE—PONT DU GARD—ATTRIBUTED TO THE EMPEROR AGRIPPA, A.D. 14

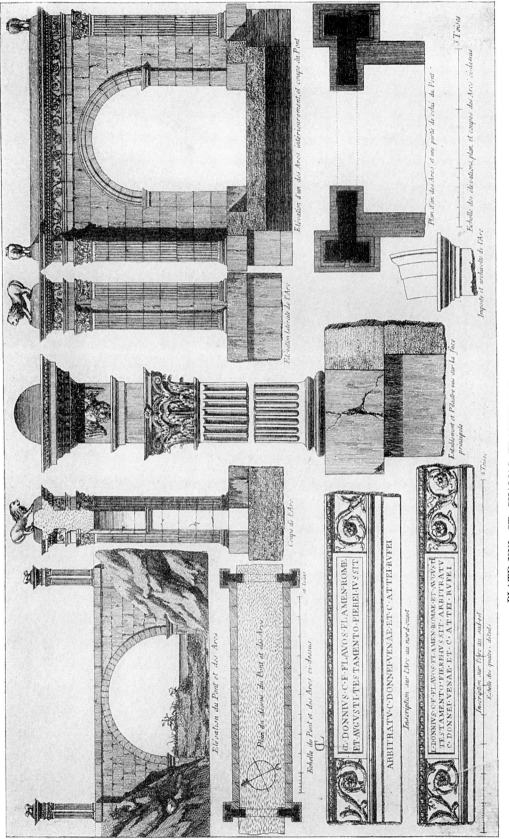

PLATE XVI—ST. CHAMAS, FRANCE—ROMAN MEMORIAL BRIDGE

FROM AN OLD ENGRAVING BY J. B. GUIBERT

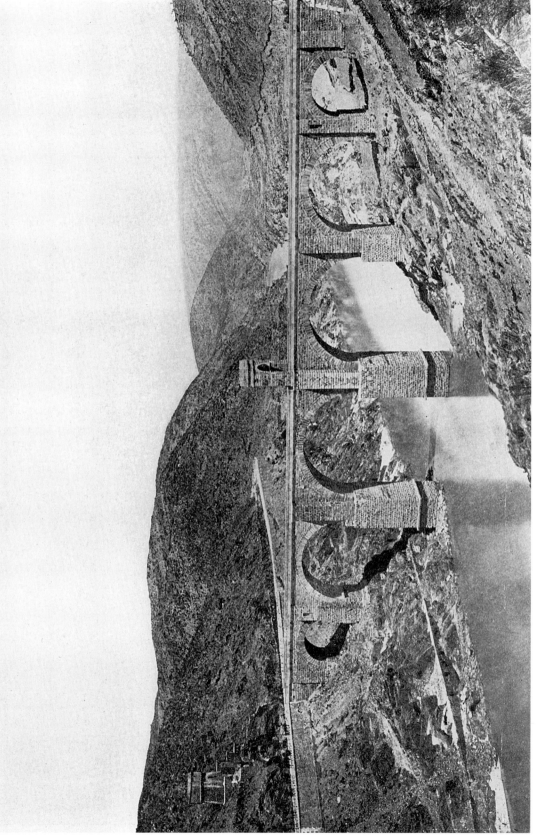

PLATE XVII—ALCANTARA, SPAIN—EL PUENTE ROMANO—CAIUS JULIUS LACER, ARCHITECT, ABOUT 98 A.D.

PHOTO BY J. LAURENT, MADRID

PLATE XVIII—SEGOVIA, SPAIN—ROMAN AQUEDUCT—BUILT ABOUT 98 A.D.
COPYRIGHT BY PUBLISHERS PHOTO SERVICE, NEW YORK

PLATE XIX—SEGOVIA, SPAIN—DETAIL OF ROMAN AQUEDUCT—BUILT ABOUT 98 A.D.

PHOTO BY LOUIS LA BEAUME

PLATE XX—SEGOVIA, SPAIN—ROMAN AQUEDUCT—BUILT ABOUT 98 A.D.

III. THE MIDDLE AGES

Pont St. Benezet, Avignon

After the fall of the Roman Empire no bridges of importance were built in Europe until about the twelfth century, at which period some of the most notable medieval structures were erected. One of the most famous of these, as well as one of the first and the largest, is the old bridge at Avignon, built in 1177-1178 by St. Benezet, containing twenty-two masonry arches, of which but four remain. The second pier supports a chapel in which repose his ashes. The design is rather crude, consisting of arch rings of uniform thickness, with solid spandrels, pierced only over the piers and carrying no ornamentation outside of the chapel, but the bridge was a noble work for those days, being about 900 meters in total length. Excepting as to length, this structure is far inferior to the Roman Bridges. (Plate XXI.)

Nearly all of the bridges of this period were built by the priests, and especially by the Benedictine Monks, who were known as "The Brothers of the Bridge." This order of the "Brothers of the Bridge" (Fratres Pontifices) was formed in the twelfth century for the purpose of maintaining hospices at bridges and important ferries or river crossings. It was recognized by Pope Clement III in 1189, and became a powerful order, building and maintaining many bridges. In fact, this priestly order represented about all the bridge building knowledge and skill that existed in Europe during several hundred years.

Traveling was dangerous during those centuries, the roads and especially the river fords being beset with robbers. The protection of travelers became one of the duties of the religious orders, and the river crossings became the sites of shelters or hospices for travelers. The work of replacing the dangerous fords and ferries with bridges naturally followed.

What witnesses of historical events these old bridges have been! Most of them have been the scenes of desperate battles, and many have suffered more from human combat than from nature. From their parapets men without number have been thrown to the streams below, sometimes for no greater offense than that their religious views differed from those of their captors. Most important bridges were fortified, and some, like that at Avignon, had roadways purposely narrowed at certain points so that two vehicles could not pass at those places, thus making their defense easier. And, indeed, in those rough, troubled times there was reason for such precautions.

Some of these old bridges retain, by name or legend, the records of these ancient battles and massacres, such as the window in the guard room of the old bridge at Orthez (constructed in the fourteenth century), which is still called "the Priests' Window" because the Protestant soldiers under Montgomery who took the town by assault in 1569 are said to have forced the priests and monks to jump into the river from this window.

One of the best examples of medieval art in fortified bridge construction is the Valentre' Bridge over the River Lot at Cahors, France, built in the early part of the fourteenth century and comprising six arches of equal span, with solid spandrels, recessed arch rings, and pointed cutwaters carried to the full height of the spandrel walls and supporting castellated parapets and three high and graceful towers. In these towers every defensive device used in the warfare of those days was provided, including slots for the crossbow-men and convenient ledges for the hurlers of missiles and pourers of burning oil.

It is truly a beautiful structure as well as a fine example of a medieval fortified bridge. Considerable restoration of this structure was found necessary in the early nineteenth century. (Plate XXII.)

Other interesting French bridges of the Middle Ages are found at St. Generoux where there is a thirteenth century bridge over the Thouet, consisting of five arch spans; at Airvault, the site of a structure of eleven fine arches dating from the twelfth century; at Orthez, where stands a bridge, the chief feature of which is a graceful center defensive tower built in the thirteenth century, and at Montauban on the Tarn where there is a fine brick bridge constructed in the fourteenth century, known as the Pont des Consuls and possessing a delightfully mellow color imparted to it by the old brick of which it is composed.

Funds to construct the bridge at Montauban were raised by a tax on visitors to the town. (Plate XXIII.)

All of these bridges are well illustrated in "Old Bridges of France," by Emerson & Gromort.

While these structures were being built in Europe, there were a number of large bridges constructed in Persia, notably at Ispahan. One of these, known as the Allah Verdi Kahn, over the Zayendeh Rud, is 350 meters long and carries a 9.1 meter roadway. Another, the Pul-i-Khajn, is 137 meters long and has a 7.3 meter roadway. Both belong to the reign of the Shah Abbas II, and to the seventeenth century.

The most important and famous structure belonging to this period was the old London Bridge, replaced by the existing structure in 1831, for many centuries of English history the only bridge across the Thames at London. A bridge has been maintained at this site since the days of King Ethelred, and it is recorded that one was destroyed in 994 in a war between the Londoners and Danes. When Canute invaded England in 1015 he found this structure in his way and dug a canal around its south end in order to complete his blockade of the city, which he was unable to capture. The bridge was destroyed again in 1091 and rebuilt by William Rufus in 1097. The latter structure was in turn destroyed by fire fifty years later. It was found so costly to maintain this timber bridge that it was determined to build one of stone, and work was begun by one Peter, the chaplain of St. Mary's Colechurch, in the year 1176. This ancient structure was founded upon piles supporting a grillage of plank on which the masonry was laid. According to the records, "not less than

33 years were occupied in the erection of this important structure. It was begun in the reign of Henry II, carried on through that of Richard I, and finished in the eleventh year of King John, 1209. Before then, however, the aged priest, its architect, died and was buried in the crypt of the chapel which had by that time been erected over the center pier. At his death, another priest, a Frenchman called Isembert, who had displayed much skill in constructing the bridges at Saintes and Rochelle, was recommended by the King as Peter's successor. But this appointment was not confirmed by the Mayor and the citizens of London who deputed three of their own body to superintend the completion of the work, the chief difficulties connected with which had indeed already been surmounted.

"That it possessed the elements of stability and strength was sufficiently proved by the fact that upon it the traffic of London was safely borne across the river for more than six hundred years. But it was an unsightly mass of masonry, so far as the bridge was concerned, although the overhanging buildings extending along both sides of the roadway, the chapel on the center pier, and the adjoining drawbridge, served to give it an exceeding picturesque appearance.

"The piers of the bridge were so close, and the arches so low, that at high water they resembled a long series of culverts hardly deserving the name of arches. The piers were of various dimensions, in some cases almost as thick as the spans of the arches which they supported were wide.

"This great obstruction of the stream had the effect of producing a series of cataracts at the rise and fall of each tide, so what was called 'The roar of the bridge' was heard a long way off.

"The feat of 'shooting the bridge' was in those days attended with considerable danger, and explains the old proverb that 'London Bridge was made for wise men to go over and fools to go under.'

"At the ends of the bridge were the gate houses, on the south one of which (until a comparative recent period) the grim heads of traitors and unfortunate partizans were stuck upon poles.

"The bridge had a long history and many vicissitudes. It had scarcely been completed ere the timber houses upon it were consumed by a great fire, but they were shortly after erected in even more cumbrous form than before. At a very early period, the bridge showed signs of weakness and required constant patching. In 1281 five arches with the buildings over them were carried away in a flood. At a subsequent period Stone's Gate, tower and arches at the southward side also fell into the river. Generation after generation of toiling men and women passed over the bridge, wearing its tracks deep with their feet, and sometimes moistening them with their tears. Still the old bridge stood on, almost down to our own day; until at last the old structure, which had served its purpose so long, was condemned and taken down, and the magnificent new London Bridge erected in its stead." (Samuel Smiles.)

It is said that the constant repairs required to maintain this bridge became so notorious that they were immortalized by being incorporated into folk lore and even now our children play to the tune of the old ditty "London Bridge is falling down." (Plate XXIV.)

It is also said in English folk lore, that "London Bridge is founded upon wool sacks," derived from the fact that its construction was partly financed through a tax on wool. In time, this statement became popularly accepted as a constructional fact.

San Martin and Alcantara Bridges, Toledo, Spain

For the best illustrations of the work of the succeeding century, the thirteenth, it is necessary to go to Spain, to Toledo, where two fine old bridges are to be found, both of them built, or rebuilt, by the Spaniards soon after the reconquest of the city from the Moors, and probably on the foundations of older Roman structures, but both decidedly Moorish in character, due perhaps to the fact that the Moors continued to be the skilled artisans of Spain for centuries after the reconquest by the Christians.

Both of these bridges are often attributed to the Roman Period.

They are named the Puente de San Martin, built in 1212 and rebuilt in 1390, and the Puente de Alcantara, originally a Roman Bridge, repaired by the Visigoths and finally rebuilt by Halaf, son of Mahomet Alameiri' in 871, and restored in 1258 by a certain D. Alfonso, after a severe flood had destroyed most of it, as recorded upon a marble slab still in place above the point of the arch. Further repairs were made to the Alcantara in 1380 and again to the towers in 1484. Regarding the restoration of the San Martin in

1390, the following story of human interest is told by George Edmund Street. (Gothic Architecture in Spain, 1865.)

"The Architect perceived that his new arch would fall down as soon as the centering was removed. Panic stricken, he went home and consulted his wife. What could she do to save her husband's reputation? She set fire to the scaffolding and destroyed the arch. The next time the Architect was wiser and did his work better. However, the lady could not keep her secret, and it is related that the Archbishop Tenorio, upon hearing of her action, did not punish her or her husband, but only congratulated the Architect upon the possession of such a faithful wife."

Both of these bridges at Toledo are fortified with massive towers at each end. San Martin has five arches, the main arch having a span of 42.7 meters. The height above the river Tagus is about 29 meters. The arches are slightly pointed and have a projecting extradosal course. One of the gateways is distinctly Moorish. The Alcantara has only two spans and is of somewhat more massive and more rude design. It is popularly called the Roman Bridge. (Plates XXV, XXVI, XXVII, XXVIII & XXIX.)

It will be noted from the photographs of these as well as of other Middle Age bridges, that the cutwaters or ends of the piers, and sometimes both, were often carried up to the roadway level to form recesses or additional roadway. These recesses served for traffic to pass at these places, the rest of the roadway seldom being of sufficient width to permit the passing of vehicles. They also provided convenient places for people to congregate and visit while enjoying the view, a pleasant custom that still survives on new as well as on old bridges.

An old French folk song runs thus:

"Sur le pont d'Avignon,
　L'on y danse, l'on y danse;
Sur le pont d'Avignon,
　L'on y danse tout en rond," etc.

Bridges were always popular for use as dance floors, even in Roman times.

"Devil's Bridges" and Medieval Bridge Folk Lore

Throughout Europe there are many so-called "Devil's Bridges," and the various folk stories connected with these bear a curious resemblance. Usually these bridges were supposed to have been built over night by the devil, and his satanic majesty, in return for his work, had demanded the first life that passed over. Sometimes the story simply records the sacrifice of a life in the construction of the bridge. Such traditions also exist in Turkey, as shown by the following legend recorded by Sir Mark Sykes in "Dar Ul Islam."

"Many years ago workmen under their masters were set to build the bridge; three times the bridge fell, and the workmen said 'The Bridge needs a life,' and the master saw a beautiful girl accompanied by a bitch and her puppies and he said, 'We will give the first life that comes by,' but the dog and her puppies held back, so the girl was built alive into the bridge and only her hand with a gold bracelet upon it was left outside."

A similar belief exists in Northern Africa among the Moors to the effect that the old bridges contain a human body built into the masonry and that such a human sacrifice was necessary to the stability of the structure.

Is it not credible that these legends have their origin in the circumstance that most large bridges as well as other human-built structures, have always demanded a sacrifice of human life through accident or misfortune, if not through strife or barbaric sacrifice?

"Go! stand by Karnak's sculptured halls;
Count o'er in those cyclopean walls
The record of her sacrifice
One life for every stone!"—(The Building of a Church-Durward.)

Even today such legends are being started. Quite recently the author stood under the shadow of one of our new great railway bridges, over a wide American river, chatting with a native fisherman, and was quite gravely informed that four men were buried alive in its concrete piers, the exact location of each immuration being pointed out.

Most of these old, so-called "Devil's Bridges" are narrow, many of them without parapets and some with very steep approaches, ofttimes so steep as to merit the term "ladder bridges," sometimes applied to them. Possibly the inconvenient features of the design of such structures have something to do with the popular notion that the devil was in some way responsible for their existence.

One of the best known of these bridges is the Devil's Bridge over the Serchio at Lucca, Italy, built about the year 1000, comprising a main span of 36.8 meters and four flanking spans. This bridge has a roadway only 2.94 meters wide and its width over all is but 3.93 meters. The grades are too steep for vehicles, as, like most of the bridges of its type and time, it was intended for foot travel, donkeys and small carts.

The material used is blue limestone and sandstone; the arch rings are well dressed, but the spandrels are of rubble only. Weale ascribes its long life to the fact that it was founded on rock and built with unusually good mortar.

Other notable examples of this type are the bridge over the River Minho at Orense, Spain; that over the Nervia at Dolceacqua, Italy, and the Bridge of Martorelli near Barcelona, Spain. The latter has a main arch span of 41 meters with a rise of 17.3 meters. It is believed that this bridge was originally built by the Romans, and restored by the Moors about 1290 A. D.

The Puente Major at Orense over the Minho is 400 meters long, belongs to the thirteenth century and is still in daily use. The large arch has a clear span of 48.5 meters and a height of 41 meters. This structure is credited to the Bishop Lorenzo. (Plates XXX, XXXI & XXXII.)

Trezzo Arch

During the fourteenth century, there was constructed at Trezzo, in Italy, the longest span masonry arch ever attempted until modern times. This structure consisted of a single arch of 82½ meters span (Hann & Hosking) across the river Adda, with a rise of 22.3 meters, about the dimensions of the recently constructed Walnut Lane concrete arch in Philadelphia. It was completed in 1377 and served until destroyed during a war in the year 1416. Its arch was segmental in form and constructed of granite. It was never rebuilt.

The Ponte Vecchio over the Arno—Florence

This is one of the few remaining "Industrial Bridges," as bridges containing shops along the sides of the roadway are sometimes called. The old London Bridge was a notable example of this type, and many of the older Paris bridges had shops and dwellings constructed on their sides. The Ponte Vecchio belongs to the early fourteenth century and consists of three segmental arches of 27.8 to 31.4 meters span and 34.3 meters width and supports a covered gallery connecting the Pitti and the Ufizzi Palaces. This work is attributed to the architect Taddeo Gaddi, best known for his paintings and mosaics. (Plate XXXIII.)

The Charles Bridge at Prague

The Karlsbrücke over the Moldau at Prague was begun in 1357 by the Emperor Charles V and finally completed in 1503. It probably still holds the world's record for length of time under construction, 146 years. It is 607 meters in length, made up of 16 arches, the longest of which has a span of 22.7 meters. At one end of this bridge is a lofty and interesting medieval tower, while the parapet is ornamented with figures of the saints, one of which, near the center, is a statue of St. John Nepomuk, the patron saint of Bohemia, who, tradition says, was thrown off the bridge and drowned at the command of the King, to whom he refused to reveal the secrets of the confessional. (Plates XXXIV & XXXV.)

At Pavia, Italy, there is a remarkable covered bridge over the Ticino, dating from 1351-1354, and consisting of seven pointed arches of brick, the arches having spans of about 21.4 meters and a height of about 19½ meters. The architect was the Governor, Gian Galeazzo Visconti, who also founded the University of Milan and was responsible for much other contemporary architectural work. (Plate XXXVI.)

Verona and Zaragossa

The fifteenth century is almost devoid of any notable achievement in bridge construction, two of the few products of that century worthy of note being the bridge at Verona, Italy, known as the Ponte Della Pietra, and the Puente de Piedra over the Ebro at Zaragossa. (Plates XXXVII, XXXVIII, & XXXIX.)

The former is partly Roman, restored in the fifteenth century, the restored parts easily recognized by their widely different character. The latter dates from 1437 and consists of seven arch spans, segmental, plain and massive, with very heavy piers of unequal width, some of them almost as wide as the arch span. The Ponte Della Pietra at Verona is much more refined in design, consisting of five arches, segmental, of variable span and carried upon piers, no two of which are alike in dimensions or detail. The spandrels over two of these piers are pierced by openings, one of which is a large circular opening, the most distinctive feature of the structure.

A fine illustration of the Medieval spirit in bridge design is the Castelvecchio of Verona with its battlemented railing. (Plate XL.)

This picturesque bridge was completed in the year 1356. The architects were probably Jean de Ferraro and Jacques de Gozzo. The arches are 24 meters to 48.7 meters span, and the roadway width 5.5 to 6.8 meters.

We are now reaching the end of the medieval period in bridge construction, characterized mostly by rude, massive, brutal strength, but also boasting many structures of bold design, more bold in conception than the preceding Roman work, but much more crude in workmanship, and we are approaching the more refined and skilled period of the Renaissance and modern times.

We leave these ancient structures with some regret and are reminded of the dialogue between the "Brigs of Ayr" as related by the poet Burns, who puts into the mouth of the Auld Brig Sprite the prophecy that the newer one will succumb first to "flood and spate," a prophecy that eventually came true.

The Auld Brig is said to date from the reign of Alexander III, who died in 1286, and it therefore belongs to about the middle of the thirteenth century. The new Brig was built in 1788 and was destroyed by a flood in 1877 and had to be rebuilt. Where can we find finer contempt of the new for the old or a better description of a river in flood than here? (Plate XLI.)

NEW BRIG

Auld Vandal, ye but show your little mense,
 Just much about it wi' your scanty sense;
Will your poor, narrow foot-path of a street,
 Where twa wheelbarrows tremble when they meet,
Your ruined, formless bulk of stone and lime,
 Compare wi' bonny Brigs o' modern time?
There's men of taste wou'd tak the Ducat-Stream,
 Tho' they should cast the vera sark and swim,
Ere they would grate their feelings wi' the view
 O' sic an ugly, Gothic hulk as you.

AULD BRIG

Conceited gowk! puffed up wi' windy pride!
  This mony a year I've stood the flood an' tide;
And tho' wi' crazy eild I'm sair forfairn,
  I'll be a Brig when ye're a shapeless cairn!
As yet ye little ken about the matter,
  But twa-three winters will inform ye better.
When heavy, dark, continued, a'-day rains,
  Wi' deepening deluges o'er-flow the plains;
When from the hills where springs the brawling Coil,
  Or stately Lugar's mossy fountains boil,
Or where the Greenock winds his moorland course
  Or haunted Garpal draws his feeble source,
Arous'd by blust'ring winds an' spotting thowes;
  In many a torrent down his snaw-broo rowes;
While crashing ice, borne on the roaring spate,
  Sweeps dams, an' mills, an' Brigs, a' to the gate;
And from Glenbuck, down to the Ratton-key,
  Auld Ayr is just one lengthened, trembling sea;
Then down ye'll hurl, deil nor ye never rise
  And dash the gumlie jaups up to the pouring skies.
A lesson sadly teaching, to your cost,
  That Architecture's noble art is lost!

NOTE:
  *Ducat-stream—a ford; mense—good manners; eild—
  age; cairn—wreck; rowes—rolls; the gate—road or way;
  Ratton-key—"Rat-hole"—a landing place at the river's
  mouth.*

Another Scottish Bridge, although of a somewhat later date and also famed in song, is the "Auld Brig of Doon." (Plate XLII.)

At Biddeford, England, an old bridge of uncertain age, but probably belonging to the fourteenth century, is of peculiar interest in that it presents the unusual spectacle of the use of the arch and beam principles combined in a single structure and material. The roadway is carried on masonry arches and the walks on stone lintels. (Plate XLIII.) This bridge formerly supported a chapel from which indulgences were sold by Grandison, Bishop of Exeter, in order to obtain funds to complete the structure.

Medieval Engineering

Following the fall of the Roman Empire and the decay of Roman civilization, engineering skill sank to a comparatively low level, and throughout the Middle Ages continued to be almost non-existent.

To be sure, wonderful churches and fine palaces were built during this period in Europe, but the skill displayed in their construction was the skill of the craftsman and not the careful, accurate planning of the engineer, as exhibited in the earlier Roman structures and later in the eighteenth century.

The civilization of the Middle Ages, based upon the feudal system, was not conducive to the development of engineering skill. The cities were more or less independent military strongholds, having little civil intercourse with each other and consequently small need of improved highways and the bridges that form a part thereof. Other branches of engineering were also neglected, and sanitation was almost unknown. As a result there were frequent pestilences that decimated the population.

On the other hand, slavery disappeared and such structures as were erected were the work of free men, a notable characteristic of the period being the development of the craftsmen's guilds, which gradually became powerful organizations.

PLATE XXI—AVIGNON, FRANCE—PONT ST. BENEZET—COMPLETED 1178

PHOTO FROM RAU STUDIOS, PHILADELPHIA

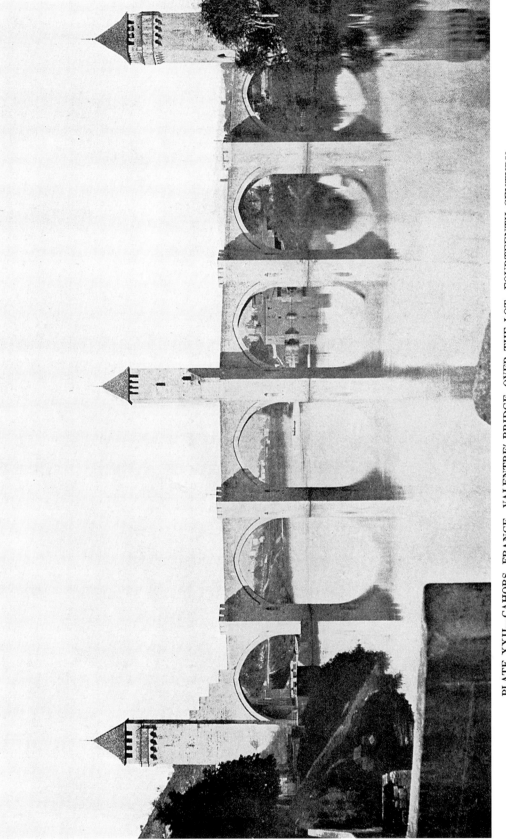

PLATE XXII—CAHORS, FRANCE—VALENTRE' BRIDGE, OVER THE LOT—FOURTEENTH CENTURY

PHOTO BY NEURDEIN FRÈRES, PARIS

PLATE XXIII—MONTAUBAN, FRANCE—PONT DES CONSULS OVER THE TARN—XIVTH CENTURY
A MEDIEVAL BRIDGE OF BRICK

PHOTO BY NEURDEIN FRÈRES, PARIS

PLATE XXIV—LONDON—THE OLD LONDON BRIDGE—PHILIP OF COLECHURCH, ARCHITECT, 1209

FROM A DRAWING BY H. W. BREWER, IN "OLD LONDON ILLUSTRATED"

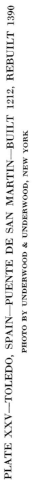

PLATE XXV—TOLEDO, SPAIN—PUENTE DE SAN MARTIN—BUILT 1212, REBUILT 1390

PHOTO BY UNDERWOOD & UNDERWOOD, NEW YORK

PLATE XXVI—TOLEDO, SPAIN—PUENTE DE SAN MARTIN—BUILT 1212, REBUILT 1390

PHOTO BY UNDERWOOD & UNDERWOOD, NEW YORK

PLATE XXVII—TOLEDO, SPAIN—PUENTE DE SAN MARTIN—DETAIL

PLATE XXVIII—TOLEDO, SPAIN—PUENTE DE ALCANTARA—REBUILT 13TH AND 17TH CENTURIES

PHOTO COPYRIGHTED BY PUBLISHERS PHOTO SERVICE, NEW YORK

PLATE. XXIX—TOLEDO, SPAIN—PUENTE DE ALCANTARA—DETAIL OF MAIN ARCH—ORIGINALLY ROMAN,
REBUILT IN THIRTEENTH AND SEVENTEENTH CENTURIES

PHOTO FROM PUBLISHERS PHOTO SERVICE

PLATE XXX—ORENSE, SPAIN—ANCIENT BRIDGE OVER THE MINHO, CREDITED TO BISHOP LORENZO, 1230

PHOTO FROM PUBLISHERS PHOTO SERVICE, NEW YORK

PLATE XXXI—DOLCEACQUA, ITALY—"THE DEVIL'S BRIDGE"—MEDIEVAL BRIDGE OVER THE NERVIA
PHOTO BY UNDERWOOD & UNDERWOOD, NEW YORK

PLATE XXXII—MARTORELLI, SPAIN—THE DEVIL'S BRIDGE—ROMAN, REBUILT BY MOORS, ABOUT 1290

PHOTO BY PUBLISHERS PHOTO SERVICE, NEW YORK

PLATE XXXIII—FLORENCE, ITALY—PONTE VECCHIO—TADDEO GADDI, ARCHITECT—FOURTEENTH CENTURY

PHOTO FROM PUBLISHERS PHOTO SERVICE, NEW YORK

PLATE XXXIV—PRAGUE—KARLSBRÜCKE

PLATE XXXV—PRAGUE—KARLSBRÜCKE—THE POWDER TOWER
PHOTO FROM THE DETROIT PUBLISHING CO.

PLATE XXXVI—PAVIA, ITALY—PONTE SUL TICINO—1354—GOVERNOR GIAN GALEAZZO VISCONTI, ARCHITECT

PHOTO BY ED. BROGI, FLORENCE

PLATE XXXVII—VERONA, ITALY—PONTE DELLA PIETRA—ROMAN AND FIFTEENTH CENTURY

PHOTO FROM ED. BROGI

PLATE XXXVIII—VERONA, ITALY—PONTE DELLA PIETRA—DETAIL—ROMAN AND FIFTEENTH CENTURY

PHOTO FROM UNDERWOOD & UNDERWOOD, NEW YORK

PLATE XXXIX—ZARAGOSSA, SPAIN—PUENTE DE PIEDRA—1437

PLATE XL—VERONA, ITALY—CASTELVECCHIO, DETAIL—1356—JEAN DE FERARE & JACQUES DE GOZZO, ARCHITECTS

PHOTO FROM M. PAUL SE'JOURNE'

PLATE XLI—SCOTLAND—THE TWA BRIGS O'AYR—THE NEW BRIG COMPLETED 1789, DESTROYED 1878, AND REBUILT

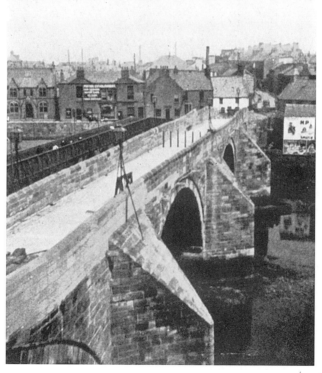

THE AULD BRIG BUILT IN THE THIRTEENTH CENTURY—RESTORED 1912

PLATE XLII—SCOTLAND—THE AULD BRIG O' DOON

PLATE XLIII—BIDDEFORD, ENGLAND—OLD MASONRY BRIDGE—PROBABLY FOURTEENTH CENTURY

PHOTO FROM WIDE WORLD PHOTOS

IV. THE RENAISSANCE PERIOD

The Renaissance, which characterized the art and architecture of the fifteenth and sixteenth centuries, seems to have had little effect upon bridge design in the fifteenth century, although during this period Brunellesco was building the Church of San Lorenzo and the Pitti Palace in Florence, and Alberti was constructing the Palace Rucellai. Possibly the thought of the time did not extend to problems of transportation, of which bridges are an important part.

In the sixteenth century, however, the effect of the Renaissance is seen in many fine bridge structures, designed and built by some of the noted architects of the period, such as The Trinity Bridge at Florence, by B. Ammanati, the Rialto and The Bridge of Sighs at Venice, both by Antonio da Ponte, contemporary of Michael Angelo and of Palladio.

Andrea Palladio was an Italian architect of the sixteenth century who designed many important buildings, but who is best known as the author of a classic treatise on architecture. In this book we find the following inspiring statement: "Bridges ought to have the self-same qualifications that we judge necessary in all other buildings, that they should be commodious, beautiful and lasting."

The Rialto Bridge, Venice

The Ponte di Rialto, over the Grand Canal, completed in 1591, consists of a single segmental arch of 51.7 meters span and has a width of 23.6 meters. It is a covered bridge, carrying a seven-arched arcade, the center arch of the arcade larger and higher than the others, and protected by a gabled roof. (Plate XLIV.)

Bridge of Sighs

The Ponte di Sospire, or Bridge of Sighs, is so named because it connects the Ducal Palace, or Court of Justice, with the jail. It is doubtless the most photographed and most painted bridge in all the world. It is a single arch of elliptical design, carrying a covered passageway, highly ornamented with human heads and cartouches, and surmounted by a heavy arched parapet. It is generally conceded that neither of these structures are worthy examples of Renaissance Art because they are inferior in design to contemporary work in buildings. The Bridge of Sighs was completed in 1597. (Plate XLV.)

Trinity Bridge, Florence

A better designed structure, perhaps, is the Trinity Bridge at Florence, built about 1570 and consisting of three basket-handled arches with rather steep approaches and embellished with statues and carved keystones. The spans are 29.3 meters and 26.2 meters. Some authorities have criticized the design of the piers of this bridge as being too thick in proportion to the rest of the structure. (Plate XLVI.)

For a good example of renaissance architecture in bridges, we must look to the seventeenth century, a period that witnessed a distinct advance in pleasing design, although but little progress in the scientific principles involved.

For instance, we have at Chatsworth, England, an ornamental little bridge built about 1668 and consisting of three arch spans, exquisitely detailed, the cutwaters of the two center piers carrying statues and the parapet consisting of an open balustrade. Certainly this little bridge is an architectural gem, if not of much importance for purposes of transportation. Evidently, its charm is due largely to its surroundings, as it is part of a beautiful country seat. (Plate XLVII.)

At Paris, however, are three notable bridges over the Seine belonging to this period, the Pont Neuf, the Pont Royal, and the Pont Marie, all serving as important links in heavily traveled arteries.

The Pont Neuf, Paris

The Pont Neuf was begun in 1578, the first stone being laid by Henry III. It was completed in 1604 and is still called the "New Bridge." Although this bridge has since that time been largely rebuilt, the restoration is an exact one. Its length is 353 meters and the width 23.6 meters. The spans of the twelve arches vary from 14 to 17.55 meters. The arch rings are three centered, nearly elliptical, and the piers have pointed cutwaters, surmounted by circular pilasters, which are carried up to the roadway, forming circular recesses in the foot-walks. The general effect of these details is to increase the appearance of massive construction.

This monumental structure, "the Patri-

arch of Paris bridges," was constructed by the architects Marchand and Androuet. (Plate XLVIII.)

The Pont Royal, Paris

The Pont Royal has five arches, the largest one with a span of 23½ meters. The width is 17 meters. It was completed in 1689 by the architects M. Mansart and J. Gabriel with the assistance of one Francois Romain from Holland, who is said to have been the first to employ open caissons or boxes, for constructing underwater foundations. "The bridge, while of the utmost simplicity in form, and without a vestige of decoration, nevertheless holds the attention of everyone whose eyes are open to the beauty of proportion." (Emerson and Gromort.)

The arches are elliptical in form and the cutwaters are triangular, surmounted with pyramidal caps reaching almost to the coping. There are no recesses, however, in the roadway. (Plates XLIX & L.)

The Pont Marie, Paris

The Pont Marie was completed in 1635 and named after its builder, M. Christophè Marie, who completed it at his own expense, receiving as compensation therefor a grant of the unbuilt section of the island. (Isle de Paris.) It consists of five nearly semi-circular arches of cut stone. Two arches were washed out in 1658, and except for this, the bridge has served traffic nearly 300 years without cessation and with slight repairs. Its first stone was laid in 1614 by Louis XIII and Marie de Medici. This bridge at one time supported houses on its sides, and it is recorded that 120 persons were drowned when two arches were destroyed in 1658, and all of the remaining houses were torn down in 1788. The width is 23.6 meters.

The bridges of Paris constitute a pleasing ensemble not equaled anywhere else in the world. This effect is due partly to the beauty of the structures themselves, but largely to the skill with which they have been made to fit into the surroundings, the approaching highways and the masonry quay walls. (Plates LI & LII.)

Charles Mulford Robinson, in "Modern Civic Art," expresses this and other attributes and requirements of good bridge design so well that we take the liberty of making the following quotation from his writings:

"In the case of a stream, bridges must form a very important feature of the water-front development, merely considered architecturally and scenically. The bridges that spring from the quays of Paris seem an inseparable part of the construction. It happens that they are separable, and rarely coincident in date with it; but this does not appear. The bridge that begins and ends in the quay must harmonize with the quay; and the quay must provide, in broadened plaza and hospitality to converging streets, a bridge approach that shall be at once suitable and convenient for the travel. The surface appearance of the bridge belongs to another discussion. We are here considering the town's water approach, where only a lateral view of the bridge is offered— the one view, however, that adequately gives the structure's architectural value; and with its art importance alone is there now concern, engineering merit is assumed.

"Stone construction, or at least stone piers, are obviously invited strongly by the masonry of the embankment in order to secure harmony. Beyond this, the charm of the bridge will lie mainly in long horizontal reaches. Perpendicular motives will not be necessary, and though it is quite the fashion, in the rare cases of an effort to make bridges monumental, to put a tower, or towers, in the centre, there is always a danger that these will have an isolated appearance. The place for the monumental treatment is at the point on the shore which is to be emphasized as the water gate; but the bridge, if designed conscientiously as a work of art that shall be permanent, as cities go, and always very conspicuous, may be made a thing of beauty with no such piling on of ornamentation. Of course at times the necessity for a centre draw justifies, and even requires, perpendicular motives; but these need not be deliberately invited to make the bridge imposing. If they are invited, the ideal place for them is at the structure's end. There they may easily emphasize the portal significance which all bridges have when the water which they span forms the boundary of the town. Interesting examples of this effect are offered by, for instance, the Charles Bridge at Prague (See Plates XXXIV & XXXV), and the railroad bridge at Mayence. (See Plate CXXVIII.) In fact, of the latter it has been remarked that while the bridge is of the very ordinary truss type, the architects have saved it aesthetically by providing 'a handsome and imposing, not to say romantic, entrance, which not even railroad tracks can ruin.' Further than that, it is an entrance, we may note, that has meaning.

"There are other principles which will be useful as guides in choosing bridge designs that are likely to please. Not only should the structure harmonize, as far as possible, with the quays and with its general setting, not only should its beauty be sought mainly in long horizontal reaches,—to the distrust of perpendicular effects, using the latter at the bridge ends if at all (when this is possible), but it must be remembered that the beauty of the bridge as a whole depends mostly on its main lines. Any attempt to deceive as to the nature and position of these by concealing them with ornament can only fail, being false to every principle of art. To beauty of form in these main lines, there must then be added symmetry.

"Imagine a stone bridge of several arching spans. It is not enough that the lines of these spans be lovely. There must be symmetry between the spans themselves, so that, for example, on either side of the center they shall be equal in number and size—an obvious matter, and yet one often ignored. And the bridge must harmonize with its natural setting and its purpose as well as with its constructed terminal. This applies to the degree of its massiveness, to the character of the scenery, or, if it be in the midst of a city, to the style of the architecture amid which it stands.

"Let it be recalled that while the purpose of the bridge is utilitarian there is no other structure in the city that has greater permanence, or as great a prominence, for good or ill. There is nothing that should be built with more consideration for the artistic result. Indeed, is it not true that a bridge across the Thames in London is upon the same plane of monumental and architectural importance as is St. Paul's itself, and so makes demand for the like skill and taste to design and to embellish it? The Romans, who were the great bridge-builders of antiquity, had no higher title to bestow than the term 'Pontifex Maximus'—greatest builder of bridges. And to-day, in an industrial age, it may be remarked, the bridge and viaduct are to us about what the town gate was to the builders of ancient times, so that it behooves us to demand not merely strength but dignity and a civic splendor, in their construction. Every city bridge is an opportunity; and as to the smaller towns, how charming a memorial a beautiful bridge might be! The triumphal arch can be made effective only at great expense. It is a vainglorious type; while in the bridge the arch is at the service of humanity.

"A Greek Sculptor charged his pupil with having richly ornamented a statue because he 'knew not how to make it beautiful.' Beauty is dependent on a fineness of line, a chastity of form, the lack of which can be atoned for by no ornament that is superimposed, by no added decoration."

Toulouse and Chatellerault, France

There exists at Toulouse, France, a remarkable bridge over the river Garonne, begun in 1543 and finally completed between 1626 and 1632, the exact date being uncertain. The design is attributed to Nicholas Bachelier and his son. The triumphal arch at one entrance was erected by the architect Mansart.

There are seven elliptical arches, and small circular openings over all piers. It is supposed that the unfinished appearance of the voussoirs over the spandrel openings is not intentional, but that the designer intended to carve a pattern thereon. All of these arches are enlarged upon the upstream side by a device known as the "corne de vache," or cow-horned arch, consisting of flattening the curve at the face of the arch, thus forming a funnel-shaped opening at the arch face. This device is often met with in old French bridges.

At Chatellerault, also, there is a somewhat similar structure consisting of nine arch spans over the River Vienne, completed in 1611, having been under construction forty-four years. The cornes de vache on this structure are very pronounced as is also the cornice. A beautiful entrance way at one end is a feature.

This bridge is known as Le Pont des Consuls and has an average span of 22 meters. It formerly had massive towers.

Both the Toulouse and Chatellerault Bridges are well illustrated by drawings in Emerson and Gromort's "Old Bridges of France." (See Plate LIV for a good example of the use of the corne-de-vache, on the old bridge at Toulouse, France.)

Engineering of the Renaissance

A characteristic of the Renaissance period is the improvement in the construction of the substructures or foundations for bridges, as well as in the execution of the superstructure. This improvement consisted chiefly in the increasing use of wood piling and timber grillages, or platforms, for foundation purposes, already applied to many of the medieval structures, as, for instance, the old London Bridge, and in the better workmanship of the stone masons, evidencing an increasing skill on the part of the designers and workmen.

PLATE XLIV—VENICE—PONTE DI RIALTO—1591—ANTONIO DA PONTE, ARCHITECT

PHOTO BY ED. BROGI, FLORENCE

PLATE XLV—VENICE, ITALY—PONTE DI SOSPIRE—RENAISSANCE, 1597—ANTONIO DA PONTE, ARCHITECT

PHOTO BY BROGI

PLATE XLVI—FLORENCE, ITALY—PONTE DELLA TRINITÀ—B. AMMANATI, ARCHITECT—ABOUT 1570

PHOTO FROM ED. BROGI, FLORENCE

PLATE XLVII—ENGLAND, CHATSWORTH—RENAISSANCE—ABOUT 1668

PLATE XLVIII—PARIS—LE PONT NEUF—COMPLETED 1604—MARCHAND & ANDROUET, ARCHITECTS

PHOTO BY LEVASSEUR, PARIS

PLATE XLIX—PARIS—LE PONT ROYAL ET LES TUILERIES—COMPLETED 1689—M. MANSARD & J. GABRIEL, ARCHITECTS

PLATE L—PARIS, FRANCE—LE PONT ROYAL—M. MANSART & J. GABRIEL, ARCHITECTS—1689

PHOTO BY LEVASSEUR, PARIS

PLATE LI—PARIS—PONT ST. LOUIS AND L'HÔTEL DE VILLE—1861

PLATE LII—PARIS—PANORAMA OF BRIDGES

PLATE LIII—PISA, ITALY—PONTE DI MEZZO—REBUILT 1660

PHOTO FROM ED. BROGI

V. THE EIGHTEENTH CENTURY

We have seen that all through the middle ages and up to the eighteenth century, all notable bridges were designed by the priests and by architects. The professional engineer had not yet appeared in the picture, at least not as differentiated from the architect. In the eighteenth century, however, the engineer appeared on the scene, and a revolution in bridge construction took place, science becoming a principal factor in design, without displacing art at that time but by displacing only ignorance and crudity.

Chief among these men were Perronet in France, and Rennie in England, the first recognized professional bridge engineers, and both belonging to the last quarter of the eighteenth and first quarter of the nineteenth centuries. Perronet was responsible, among numerous projects, for the bridge over the Seine at Neuilly, a suburb of Paris, built 1768 to 1773, and consisting of five arches, each with a span of 39 meters, and also for the Pont de la Concorde at Paris, built 1788. The famous Loire Bridge at Orleans was built by Perronet in collaboration with Hupeau, a contemporary engineer. (Brief biographies of Rennie and of Perronet may be found in Appendix C.)

The Pont de la Concorde

The Pont de la Concorde was the first bridge in Paris to be constructed with segmental arches. It has five spans with rises of only about one-eighth the opening—bold proportions for those days. It is considered to be Perronet's masterpiece. One of its features is the use of an open balustrade, or railing, of stone posts and spindles instead of the usual solid parapet wall of its predecessors. This bridge is 15.59 meters wide between faces. The central arch has a span of 31.18 meters with a rise of 3.97 meters, the flanking arches being somewhat less. Perronet intended to use cylinder piers in the plan of the Pont de la Concorde as he had already done in the design of a bridge at St. Maxena, but the approaching revolution led him to abandon this plan in favor of the straight pier in order to speed up the work. The cutwaters are about three-quarters attached circular columns, extended to the coping and supporting heavy masonry posts probably intended as bases for statuary, but never so used. There are no recesses in the foot walks. Perronet was the first director of the Ecole des Ponts, founded by Turdaine in 1747, the first school of bridges. Perronet used the device known as the "corne-de-vache" (cow-horns) extensively and said of it: "This arrangement facilitates the introducing of the water and gives more lightness and boldness of effect to the bridge." The use of the flat segmental arch was another characteristic of his work. (Plate LV.)

Rennie is best known as the engineer for the New London Bridge, built in 1831, the Waterloo Bridge at London built in 1817, and the old Southwark Bridge of cast iron arches, built in 1819. Rennie, however, built many other creditable structures in England and Scotland. A characteristic of his bridges is the use of the elliptical arch, in order to obtain a low, level roadway, while Perronet evidently preferred to use the flat segmental arch to obtain this same result.

It will hardly be questioned that the semi-ellipse curve gives the more pleasing results, due largely to the fact that it presents to the eye a completed curve, whereas the segmental form is but part of a curve, it is incomplete. This likewise holds true for the semi-circle, which also gives the effect of a completed curve. Similarly, the simple mathematical curve has a charm not possessed by curves made up of a combination of different mathematical curves, such as we see in the three-centered and five-centered types, and in curves of varying radii, such as are commonly used today in the design of reinforced concrete bridges. When it is necessary to use the segmental type of arch, as it often is, the designer should recognize the apparent necessity for skewbacks or abutments sufficiently massive to provide for the evident thrust, to the eye, of the uncompleted arch. In general, it may be stated as a cardinal principle of design that simple and complete curves are preferable for arch rings.

These pioneer bridge engineers, Perronet and Rennie, built structures that were much more beautiful, as well as more practicable, than any of their predecessors, in any age, whether architect or priest, Roman or Medieval. Possibly this is due to the fact that engineering and architecture were still closely related, and these engineers were students of both.

The Waterloo Bridge

The Waterloo Bridge, designed by Rennie, consists of nine arch spans of elliptical shape, each span having a length of 120 feet and a rise of 34 feet. This bridge, originally called the 'Strand Bridge,' was re-named the Waterloo Bridge in honor of the battle of that name. The design, while universally admired for its beauty, has been the object of some criticism because of the use of columns at the piers, which are obviously superfluous ornamentation.

Thomas Pope, writing in "A Treatise on Bridge Architecture," thus pays his respects to this detail, perhaps somewhat unjustly, but not without point:

"Dear little columns, what is't ye do there?
We know not, sir, unless to make you stare."

Apropos of the same problem, William Hosking wrote nearly a century ago, "The usual materia architectoricae are entirely out of place, and out of character, in bridge compositions. Columns and approximation to columnar form and proportion, pilasters, entablatures, niches, battlements, balustrades, towers and turrets, pinnacles and pediments, are gauds and devices, in the application of which to bridge composition the most eminent engineer-architects have failed to produce anything but meanness or absurdity, or a combination of both.

"If a work such as a bridge be well composed constructively, whatever may be the constituent material or materials employed, and whatever may be the kind of construction, it can hardly fail to be an agreeable object for it will certainly possess the essentials to beauty in architectural composition, simplicity and harmony. The introduction of anything not necessary to the construction, the omission of what is requisite, or the substitution of a bad expedient for a good one, will assuredly tell injuriously upon the eye, how incompetent soever the observer may be to determine the cause of the defect, or even in what the defect may consist. It is impossible, therefore, to draw any line between the constructive and the decorative, or what is commonly termed the architectural composition of a bridge." (Plate LVI.)

The New London Bridge

The New London Bridge comprises five masonry arches, of elliptical shape, and is 926 feet long. The roadway, originally but 35 feet wide, was widened in 1905 to 65 feet and again in 1915 by the insertion of massive granite corbels to a width of 76 feet. This last widening was carried out by Andrew Murray, architect, and G. F. W. Cruttwell, engineer. This bridge was and still is a masterpiece of simple, yet effective design, entirely devoid of the ornamentation for which the earlier Waterloo bridge has been criticized. The piers have circular cutwaters, slightly pointed, and the spandrels are built with coursed ashlar jointed precisely to the voussoirs of the arch rings, the entire effect being one of carefully executed design and workmanship. Recesses are provided over all piers. (Plate LVII.)

These London bridges have served the heaviest traffic for over a century and only lately have they shown signs of serious distress, due chiefly to deterioration of the timber grillages or platforms supported by piling upon which the piers are founded. The same weakness is causing concern for the safety of Sir Christofer Wren's masterpiece, St. Paul's Cathedral.

Immediately after the great London fire this eminent architect, engineer and mathematician, collaborator with Sir Isaac Newton in the writing of "Principice," planned, among other improvements, to rebuild the old London Bridge, a plan that was not carried out at that time.

A picturesque bridge of the eighteenth century is the "Old Bridge" at Heidelberg, Germany, built 1786 to 1788 by the Elector Charles Theodore, whose statue, in company with one of the goddess Minerva, adorns the parapets. (Plate LVIII.)

At Chalon, France, there is a bridge of very unusual design, over the River Saone, known as the Pont St. Laurent, completed in 1782 by Emilian Marie Gauthey, a noted French engineer and author of a book on bridge construction. The plan is unsymmetrical, comprising four semi-circular arches and one segmental. The structure is ornamented with carvings in the spandrel recesses, and the arch rings are double and strongly marked, but the most remarkable detail is the extension of the triangular breakwaters to a point well above the roadway level. Another fine bridge by Gauthey is that over the Saone at Chalon, known as the Pont des Echavannes. (See "Old Bridges of France" for many fine drawings of Gauthey's work.)

Among smaller structures built in this period, one of the most famous is the Pont-Y-Pridd, in Wales, completed by a William Edwards in 1750 after two attempts had failed. This belongs to the "Devil's Bridge" type, having steep grades and narrow roadway. A peculiar feature is the provision of the openings in the spandrels. The span is 140 feet. It is said that Edwards' father was drowned at this point and that the building of the bridge was in fulfillment of a vow made by the son at that time. The more modern low grade bridge alongside this old structure affords a marked contrast between the old and the new. (Plate LIX.)

Before leaving the eighteenth century we should not forget to mention the masonry arch bridges built by Smeaton at Perth, at Banff, and at Coldstream in Scotland, all quite similar in design to Rennie's work and belonging to the latter part of the eighteenth century.

An important factor in the construction of all masonry bridges in all times has been the quality of the cementing or jointing material used. As we have already noted, much of the old Roman work was laid up without mortar joints, dependence being placed upon careful dressing of the abutting beds of the stones, at which their workmen were very expert. The Romans, however, knew how to manufacture an excellent cement which they used freely in mortar and in concrete for much of their bridge construction. The art of making this cement was lost for a thousand years during the middle or dark ages.

Smeaton, the engineer in charge of the design and construction of the Eddystone Lighthouse, quite a famous engineering feat in its day, conducted some studies and experiments in connection therewith which led to his re-

discovery of so-called Natural Cement in 1756.

In 1824, another English engineer, Joseph Aspdin, made the first Portland Cement, distinguished from the natural kind by being made from a mixture of raw materials, a discovery that made possible the modern concrete bridges, which have almost revolutionized the art of bridge architecture.

An old saying of Scotch masons runs thus:

"When a hundred years are past and gane, then gude mortar is grown to stane."

Eighteenth Century Engineering

The eighteenth century marked the re-birth of civil engineering as a science. After a dormant period covering nearly 1500 years, good roads began again to be constructed throughout Europe, improved harbors were built, water works and canals constructed and a start made at sanitation. Bridge construction became more scientific, foundations were better prepared than ever before, the use of the open cofferdam for building in deep water was introduced and universally adopted, better cement was manufactured and all parts of the work show a marked improvement in workmanship, materials and tools.

This was all coincident with a general advance in scientific knowledge, on which the engineering profession is necessarily founded, and the establishment of schools for the training of scientists and engineers; developments that made possible the tremendous material achievements of the nineteenth century.

PLATE LIV—TOULOUSE, FRANCE—"THE OLD BRIDGE"—1542-1632
ILLUSTRATING THE USE OF THE "CORNE-DE-VACHE"
PHOTO FROM "GRANDES VOUTES" SÉJOURNÉ

PLATE LV—PARIS—LE PONT DE LA CONCORDE—1787—M. PERRONET, ENGINEER

PLATE LVI—LONDON—WATERLOO BRIDGE OVER THE THAMES—JOHN RENNIE, ENGINEER—1817

PLATE LVII—LONDON—NEW LONDON BRIDGE AS BUILT, 1831—JOHN RENNIE, ENGINEER

PLATE LVIII—HEIDELBERG, GERMANY—1788

PLATE LIX—WALES—THE PONT Y PRIDD—1750—WM. EDWARDS, BUILDER—SPAN 140 FEET

VI. THE MODERN ERA

The advent of the railroad era, dating from the completion of the Manchester and Liverpool Railway by George Stevenson, about 1830, marked the beginning of the modern era of bridge construction, and gave a tremendous impetus to the science thereof. Prior to this era, bridges were built more as a convenience than as a necessity, as fords or ferries could be used by most of the vehicles then in use. The railroad locomotive, however, cannot ford a stream, and bridges became an absolute necessity. Unfortunately, the desire for both speed of construction and economy was so great that nearly all consideration of beauty was soon lost sight of, utility only receiving attention in the design of most railroad bridges, resulting in the disfiguration of the landscape in many instances. In recent years, however, a reaction from this barbaric materialism has set in and some of our most pleasing modern bridges are railroad structures.

The requirements of the railroad era also caused a great change in the materials used in bridge construction, the need for long spans that could not be built with masonry arches leading to the rapid adoption of iron, both cast and wrought, and later of steel. These changes also resulted in the development of other types of bridges besides the arch; the iron beam or girder, the suspension bridge, the cantilever and the truss, including the trussed, or braced arch, came into use. In fact, modern bridge design makes free use of all of the five basic mechanical principles, the simple beam, the cantilever, the arch, the suspension cord, and the truss, whereas, prior to the last century, the arch was almost the only principle used for large bridges, the beam being used for very short and unimportant spans, and the suspension principle used only to a limited extent.

Robert Stevenson, the designer of the railroad locomotive, and engineer of many early railroads, was also the designer of three great bridges, and many lesser ones. These three bridges are the Britannia Bridge, carrying the Chester and Holyhead Railway over the Straits of Menai, in North Wales; the high level Bridge at Newcastle over the Tyne, and the Victoria Bridge over the St. Lawrence at Montreal, Canada, the superstructure of which has since been replaced by modern trusses.

The Britannia Bridge

The Britannia Bridge, Wales, completed in 1850, is a wrought iron tubular girder, the trains passing through the tubes. It is 1511 feet long, in one continuous tube, the longest single span being about 550 feet between supports. The piers, built of sandstone faced with marble, were designed to carry suspension chains, which were included in the original design, but later omitted. Colossal lions guard the bridge heads, the work of Mr. John Thomas, an English sculptor. Originally it was intended to place a colossal figure of Britannia over the center pier, but this was never done. The general effect is grand and simple, but marred by the unused provision in the towers for suspenders. The Britannia Bridge was the first large example of wrought iron construction, no cast iron being used. It contains 11,468 tons of wrought iron, a stupendous tonnage for those days. (Plate LX.)

⸰ ⸰ ⸰

The Bridge at Newcastle is 1372 feet long, composed of six major openings each 125 feet in the clear, spanned by iron bowstring girders carrying an upper and lower deck. Robert Stevenson was the first engineer to use this type of truss.

⸰ ⸰ ⸰

The Victoria Bridge was built to carry the Grand Trunk Railway over the St. Lawrence River near Montreal, at a point where the river is about 1¾ miles wide and was similar to the Britannia Bridge in design.

Robert Stevenson, one of the greatest of the world's engineers, largely responsible for the development of the railroad, was also one of the leading industrialists of his day, and his regard for his workmen is well illustrated by the remark he once made that "Skilled labor is the great fulcrum upon which all our social progress depends." He might well have included artistic progress, also.

It is significant that at the beginning of the nineteenth century there was a widespread general interest in the building of iron bridges. Among others, the famous sceptic, Tom Paine, was an ardent advocate of the iron bridge, and built, at his own expense, an experimental arch of 88½-foot span, as a demonstration, and later was responsible for the design of an iron bridge over the Wear near Sunderland, constructed in 1796 and containing a span of 236 feet. Paine's work was weak, however, and had to be rebuilt by Stevenson, not the only instance of correction, by the engineer, of the layman's constructional errors.

Prof. Pole in writing of the Britannia Bridge in 1866, closes his description with the following pertinent observation:

"The unfettered reign of private enterprise, which, under the dictatorship of the engineer, has of late so much prevailed in this country, has been no doubt a grand source of works of commercial utility, but it has doomed us to much bitter humiliation in matters of art and taste."

That reign has not yet ended but is beginning to yield to a new era which recognizes Art as a desirable partner of Science, in Bridges, as well as in other structures.

An important factor in this change is the invention and development of reinforced concrete, allowing a very much wider use of this plastic masonry material than was formerly possible.*

About 1867, M. Jos. Monier began to use

---

*Concrete is not a new material. It was known to and used by the Phoenicians, the Carthaginians and the Romans, who developed it to a high state as a building material, as evidenced by the existing remains of many ancient aqueducts and buildings. Perhaps the best known example of Roman concrete construction yet standing is the dome of the Pantheon at Rome, 142 feet in diameter and about 1900 years old.

The Roman builders used a mixture of lime rock and volcanic ash or Pozzulano in the manufacture of their cement, obtaining a material superior to most natural cements, but inferior to our modern Portland Cement, which was first made in England in 1824, and received its name because of its resemblance in color to Portland stone, a well-known building stone of that name.

metal reinforcement embedded in concrete in order to increase its resistance to tensile stresses, and about 1889 the principle was applied to bridge construction by M. Hennebique in France, and shortly thereafter by Prof. Melan in Austria, and by Edwin Thacher and others in the United States.

Much of the best recent work in bridge architecture has been done in this material, as will be shown later. First, however, we will consider some recent works in stone masonry.

Stone Masonry Bridges of the Modern Period

Many very important bridges have been constructed of cut stone masonry in both Europe and America in the modern period, from 1800 to 1925, in spite of the tremendous impetus given to the use of iron and steel during this time, often called the "Age of Steel," and also to the more recent impetus given to the use of concrete by the perfection of Portland Cement, leading to the frequent use of the term "Age of Concrete," applied to recent construction.

The greater beauty and longer life of stone masonry bridges, as compared to steel, and, at least until very recent years, to concrete, have earned for stone masonry a preference as the best material for use in the construction of permanent and monumental structures. Even today many engineers consider that concrete has not yet definitely proven that it is as permanent a material as natural stone, and it is generally conceded that a concrete has not yet been developed that admits of as satisfactory a surface treatment as may be obtained by the use of natural stones, al-

though it must be admitted that much progress is being made in this respect.

Among modern European stone bridges, the following are selected as worthy of especial note:

At Paris, over the River Seine, the Pont de la Archeveche, the Pont Notre Dame, the Pont Au Change and the Pont Louis Phillippe.

At Plauen, the bridge over the Syra River; at Luxemburg, the Adolphe Bridge; at Pisa, the Ponte Solferino by Vincenzo Micheli, and at Geneva, the Coulouvrenier Bridge over the Rhone.

Among American stone structures, built during the last century, the following are perhaps most notable:

The Harlem River Aqueduct Bridge at New York, the Cabin John Aqueduct at Washington, the bridge over the Connecticut River at Hartford, Conn., and the viaduct of the Pennsylvania Railroad over the Susquehanna River near Harrisburg, Pa.

Modern Masonry Bridges over the River Seine at Paris

(Data obtained largely from the description of "The Bridges of Paris" by Carl L. Rimmele in The Military Engineer)

The Pont de la Archeveche, completed in 1828, is composed of three segmental arches of low rise as compared with the span. The central arch has a span of 17 meters, with a rise of 2.31 meters and the others 15 meters span and 1.91 meters rise. The width is 11 meters. The design is extremely plain and devoid of ornamentation. The railing is of metal with top and bottom rails and triangular pattern of webbing, very light and simple. (Plate LXI.)

The Pont Notre Dame as it exists today was rebuilt in 1852 on the foundations of an older structure built in 1499-1507 by the Joconde Brothers, an Italian religious organization. In the rebuilding of this bridge, elliptical arches were employed for the first time in Paris bridges. There are five spans, varying slightly from 18.76 meters to 17.40 meters in length, and with a rise of from 7.5 to 7.25 meters. The width is 21 meters over all. The stone masonry of the old bridge was used in rebuilding the new. The old bridge was flanked with buildings on each side and was the property of the king, who collected tolls. Similar conditions prevailed at all of the five bridges over the Seine in Paris existing in the sixteenth century.

Is it not possible that the custom of building dwelling houses on bridges so prevalent during the Middle Ages was due to the influence of a natural desire to live over water, inherited from our remote European ancestors, the Lake Dwellers, or was it simply a matter of business, the density of travel making the sites valuable for shops, and the dwellings being connected with shops, as was the custom? In modern times, it has been found that such sites are not, as a rule, desirable for business, due to the lack of room and the very congestion of travel, which is required by the modern spirit to "move on" and not stop for shopping or gossip.

The Pont Au Change, rebuilt in 1858 to 1860, also replaced an older bridge; in fact, a bridge has existed at this site since before the beginning of the Christian Era. The old bridge consisted of six spans, while the new bridge is composed of but three elliptical arches, each with 31.60 meters span and 7.22 meters rise. This bridge has the unusual width of 30 meters between parapets. In this work also, stone from the ancient structure was used in the new work. The cutwaters of the piers are circular and carried up to the extradosal lines, above which is placed a large letter "N" encircled by a wreath, the emblem of Napoleon. There is no other ornamentation. The parapets are of the post and spindle type. (Plate LXII.)

The Pont Louis Phillipe, built 1860 to 1862, is also composed of three elliptical arch spans, quite similar in dimensions to those of the Pont Au Change, the center span having a length of 32 meters and the side spans 30, with rise of 8.25 meters and 7.73 meters respectively. The Pont Au Change is supposed to occupy the site of the Grand Pont of Julius Ceasar's time. The only other Paris bridge existing at this ancient date was the Little Pont, as the more modern structure is still called.

Other bridges at Paris belonging to the last century are the Pont St. Michel, the Pont des Invalides, the Pont de l'Alma, the latter named in honor of the victory of Alma during the Crimean War in 1854. There are four figures on the pier heads of the Pont de l'Alma, representing four contemporary types of French soldiers, a kind of applied ornamentation that would seem to be proper since it conveys a significance in harmony with the memorial character of the bridge itself. This work, executed under the direction of M. de Lagalisserie, engineer, in 1855, comprises arches of 43 meters span and a width of 20 meters. (Plate LXIII.)

Also named for a military victory are the Pont d'Austerlitz, commemorating the victory of Napoleon over the Austrians, constructed in 1801 to 1805, rebuilt in 1854 and widened in 1884; and the Pont d'Iena, named for the French victory over Prussia at Iena-Auerstadt in 1806.

Iron and Steel Bridges at Paris

Paris also boasts, in addition to her wonderful masonry arch bridges, some arch bridges of cast iron notable for their beauty. Among these is the widened Pont Tournelle. The original arches are of masonry, dating back to 1654, and the roadway was widened in 1845 by addition of metallic arches on each side. Strange to say, the effect is not considered bad, a tribute to the skill of the designers.

The Pont de Carrousel is, perhaps, the best known of the metallic arch bridges of Paris. It consists of three spans of 47 meters length and a rise of one-tenth of this amount. The arch ribs are built up of wood and cast iron combined and the spandrels have circular iron rings diminishing in size toward the crown. From an engineering viewpoint, this bridge is not satisfactory and the architectural value is not much better. The deck is 12 meters wide.

The Pont d'Arcole, built in 1854, has a single wrought iron arch span of 80 meters length.

The Pont Alexandre III, completed in 1900 after plans by MM. Resal and Alby, is the most ornate of the bridges of Paris, and consists of a single metallic arch of 109 meters span and only 6.28 meters rise, a very extreme ratio of rise to span of 1/17. Somewhat lavish use of cast iron ornamentation on the exterior ribs and spandrels, huge masonry pylons at the corners and statuary surmounting secondary posts, constitute the elaborate decorative scheme. It is 40 meters wide. (Plate LXIV.)

A bridge at Plauen over the Syra River is the longest single span stone masonry arch in the world, having a clear span of 90 meters and a rise of 17 meters. The engineer in charge of this project was M. C. H. Leibold and the work was completed in 1903. It is called the Frederic August Bridge and consists of a single mammoth arch of the basket-handle curve type, with openings in the spandrels over the skewbacks and a simple arcade supporting the walks. The deck comprises a roadway 11 meters wide and two walks each 3 meters wide. Dentils are used under the coping, which supports a simple stone parapet. (Plate LXXVIII.)

The Luxemburg Bridge is considered to be a handsomer structure than that of Plauen, and contains an arch nearly as long, 84.5 meters, and with the much greater height of 41.75 meters. This bridge, completed in 1903, spans the Petrusse River and consists of a single arch composed of two parallel stone masonry ribs, supporting four spandrel arches on each side of the center and flanked by two full centered arches, one on each side of the main span. The main arch ribs, for a short distance up from the skewbacks, are built of rough rock-faced masonry, which gives the effect of more massive skewbacks, against which the main arch rings of smooth-faced stone abut. The side spans each have 21.6 meters opening, and the spandrel arches 5.4 meters. The parapets are of simple spindle design, enclosing a deck having a clear width of 16 meters, comprising an 8 meter roadway, a railway track, traction track and two walks. A cartouche, the coat-of-arms of the Grand Duke of Luxemburg, ornaments the keystone. The facing material is stone masonry, but the floor is constructed of reinforced concrete.

The engineer in charge of the design and the construction of this beautiful and imposing structure was M. Séjourné, Ingenieur en Chef des Ponts et Chausses of France, who is also the author of one of the most important modern books on masonry arches—"Grandes Voutes." (Plate LXVII.)

⸗ ⸗ ⸗

A beautiful bridge at Pisa, Italy, known as the Ponte Solferino, completed in 1875 by the architect Vincenzo Micheli, consists of three elliptic arches delicately moulded and supported on piers having circular cutwaters. The only attempt at ornamentation consists of the carved keystones, cartouches in the panels over the piers and statues at the four large end posts of the post and spindle railing. (Plate LXVIII.)

⸗ ⸗ ⸗

The Coulouvrenier Bridge at Geneva, completed in 1895, is a fine example of good modern bridge construction, not nearly so delicately beautiful as the Ponte Solferino, but more massive. There are two main spans of segmental arches, one over a river and the other over a canal. Between them are two piers connected by a single semicircular arch

of short span. Surmounting these two piers are slender, high pylons, supported on carved brackets projecting from the spandrels. This central group forms the principal architectural feature of the bridge and is very effective. The arch rings are of rock-faced masonry, as are also the piers up to the brackets. The main arches have a clear span of 40 meters and the center arch an opening of 108 meters. The deck comprises a single roadway, 11 meters wide, and two walks with a clear width of 3.5 meters each. The balustrades are of granite, of the "post and spindle" type. Although this bridge is faced throughout with stone, the body of the main arches and the roadway are of concrete. The engineer was M. Constant Butticaz, and the consulting architect, M. Bonvier. (Plate LXIX.)

⸗ ⸗ ⸗

The Hannibal Bridge over the Vulturne in Italy is so named because it occupies the site of an ancient structure supposed to have been built by Hannibal. The modern structure was completed in 1870, and consists of a single segmental arch of 55 meters span, flanked with circular openings in the abutments, one on each side, of 9.71 meters span. The extradosal rings of the arches, the copings of the circular cutwaters of the piers, and the main copings, all have heavy dentils which give a very unusual character to the bridge. The engineer was M. Giustino Fiocca. A peculiarity of this bridge and some others of the more recent Italian bridges consists in the use of a segmental ring for the exposed faces of the arch, the main section of which is elliptical. (Plate LXXII.)

⸗ ⸗ ⸗

At Kew, England, is a three-span arch bridge

over the Thames, built in 1903 and named the Edward the Seventh Bridge. The arches are elliptical in section, 133 feet in span, constructed of large voussoirs, have spandrels flush with the faces of the arch rings and no ornamentation, except the large carved cartouches over the piers. The curve of the ellipse is carried down the sides of the piers, giving the latter a very heavy, but pleasing, appearance. This is a simple detail that might often be employed profitably, although the cutting of the voussoirs requires considerable skill in stereotomy. The engineer was Sir John Wolfe Barry, K. C. B. (Plate LXXIII.)

✓ ✓ ✓

Another beautiful French structure is the Pont Antoinette over the Agout at Tarn, built in 1884 for railroad purposes and consisting of a simple arch span of 50 meters with five full-centered arches each side of the center, the main arch springing from between two piers of these smaller arches. The charm of this bridge is due partly to the use of differently colored stone, a light colored stone for the main arch ring, the coping and retaining walls, while the balance is of a much darker stone, accentuating the main features. The engineer in charge was M. Robaglia. (Plate LXXIV.)

In Austria, at Vorailberg, a railroad arch bridge spans a deep gorge with a single massive arch ring of uniform thickness, supporting four spandrel arches on each side. The pleasing effect of this bridge is obtained by the use of large stones of irregular size and rough rock-faced masonry, all suggestive of rugged strength and harmonizing with the rugged character of the surrounding land-scape. The span is only 41 meters and the only parapet a pipe railing. The design is typical of many others on Austrian railways. (Plate LXXV.)

✓ ✓ ✓

At Orleans, France, over the Loire, is another railway bridge, built in 1906, consisting of seven equal spans of 43.85 meters each, of open spandrel design similar to many other structures, but distinguished by the use of brick for the spandrel walls, and also for the panels of the parapets. The contrast of color is sharp, much more so than in the case of the Pont Antoinette. The engineer in charge was M. Renardier. (Plate LXXVI.)

✓ ✓ ✓

A bridge over the Moselle, in Lorraine, completed in 1905, embraces some features of architectural design worthy of note. This structure is of the common open spandrel, segmental arch type, the distinctive features being the treatment of the pilasters over the piers with dressed stone edges and rock-faced panels and the use of a very simple metal railing with double posts over all piers and columns. The engineer was M. Blumhardt. (Plate LXXVII.)

✓ ✓ ✓

The Séjourné Bridge over the Pedrouse, named in honor of its designer, M. Paul Séjourné, consists of masonry arches 65.2 meters high and was built in 1911. It is remarkable for its great height. (Plate LXVI.)

✓ ✓ ✓

The Puente Nuevo at Ronda, Spain, a high masonry arch over a deep gorge, designed by Jose Martin Aldeguela, is a unique structure, the abutments being carried up the sides of the gorge in perpendicular lines. The architect was killed by a fall from his work while under construction. Older Roman and Moorish bridges cross this gorge at lower levels. (Plate LXXIX.)

"The High Bridge" at New York was built in 1837 to 1842 as an aqueduct for the Croton water supply system of the city under the direction of John B. Jervis, engineer. It consists of 16 full-centered (semi-circular) arches of 80 feet span each, on high piers. The total length is 1460 feet and the height above the river is 116 feet. The design is simple, the principal charm of the structure lying in its proportions and in the fine workmanship of its dressed stone masonry.

It is now (1927) found necessary to remove some of the piers of this bridge on account of interference with navigation of the river, an alteration which it is hoped will not mar its beauty. (Plate LXXX.)

The Cabin John Arch, near Washington, D. C., was completed in 1864 by General Meigs, U. S. A. This structure is part of the water system of Washington, D. C., and consists of a single arch of 220 feet opening and 101 feet rise. It is chiefly noted for its size, although a much more distinctive feature is the use of a double arch ring, the inner or lower ring of dressed stone, and an upper or extradosal ring of rock-faced stone. (Plate LXXXI.)

One of the most beautiful structures in America is a bridge over the Connecticut River at Hartford, Connecticut, completed in 1908, and known as the Memorial Bridge. The length of this bridge is 1192 feet and its width is 82 feet. The nine arches have an opening of 119 feet each, are elliptical in shape, built of cut granite, smooth faced. The piers have triangular cutwaters, the spandrels are flush with the faces of the arch rings and the coping is a simple projecting band of granite unrelieved by dentils or otherwise. The parapet is a solid wall, capped with a plain coping. There are two enlarged piers with projecting bays. Extreme simplicity is the keynote of this bridge, yet the effect is very pleasing and possibly unexcelled by any similar structure. One cannot study the architecture of the masonry bridge without being impressed with the great beauty of the elliptic curve, when used for such low-lying structures as this. The design is credited to Mr. A. P. Boller, consulting engineer, in collaboration with Mr. E. D. Graves, chief engineer, and Mr. E. M. Wheelwright, consulting architect. (Plate LXXXII.)

American Railway Stone Arches

Many fine bridges of stone masonry have been built in America by the various railroads, such as the bridge over the Susquehanna River near Harrisburg, Pa., on the Pennsylvania Railroad, consisting of a long series of equal span, semicircular, solid spandrel arches of sandstone. (Plate LXXXIII.)

On the lines of the New York Central Railroad, especially that part formerly known as the Lake Shore & Michigan Southern Railway, are many fine examples of cut-stone masonry arches, typical of which are the bridges over Black River, at Elyria, and at Berea, Ohio, both high arches having solid masonry spandrels with no earth fill. These bridges were built of the famous Berea Sandstone, found in northern Ohio, and extensively used for bridge construction, as well as for buildings.

At Elyria, Ohio, there is also an unusually flat stone highway arch, having a rise of about 28 feet, for a span of 155 feet. It was built in 1886 of Berea Sandstone, about the same time that the railway bridges mentioned were constructed. (Plates LXXXIV & LXXXV.)

At Cleveland, Ohio, are some unusual masonry bridges, built about 1900 after designs by Architect C. F. Schweinfurth and carrying city streets over the Rockefeller Parkway. The material is sandstone for the facing, although some of the arches have rings of brick. The designs are quite unique, a feature being the omission of the usual copings and parapets. (Plates LXXXVI & LXXXVII.)

Timber Bridges

In the early decades of the nineteenth century, many timber arch bridges were built in the United States. Timber was plentiful and therefore this type of structure was economical in first cost, and, indeed, many of them served nearly a century of usefulness. Little can be claimed for them as objects of beauty, yet some of them possessed a picturesque charm. Among the more famous was that over the Delaware River at Trenton, consisting of 203-foot spans, built in 1804, and replaced in 1875 by an uninteresting steel truss bridge. The Collossus Bridge over the Schuylkill at Philadelphia, quite noted at one time for its clear span of 340 feet and a rise of only 38 feet, was built in 1812 and destroyed by fire in 1838, a fate that befell many, if not most of these timber structures.

The so-called "Y" Bridge at Zanesville, Ohio, located at the junction of the Muskingum and Licking Rivers, another famous timber structure, was built about 1820 and replaced with a concrete bridge in 1900, serving this community faithfully for eighty years. The most ambitious timber arch bridge ever attempted, however, was built near Baden, Germany, in 1760 by the Brothers Grubenman, noted bridge builders of that day. This structure boasted the unprecedented length of 360 feet in a single span. (Plate LXXXIX.)

PLATE LX—WALES—BRITANNIA TUBULAR BRIDGE—1850—ROBERT STEVENSON, ENGINEER

PHOTO FROM PUBLISHERS PHOTO SERVICE, NEW YORK

PLATE LXI—PARIS—LE PONT DE LA ARCHEVECHE—BUILT 1828

PHOTO BY LEVASSEUR, PARIS

PLATE LXII—PARIS—LE PONT AU CHANGE—BUILT 1860

PHOTO BY LAVASSEUR, PARIS

PLATE LXIII—PARIS—PONT DE L'ALMA—1860

PLATE LXIV—PARIS—PONT ALEXANDRE III—MM. RESAL & ALBY, ENGINEERS—COMPLETED 1900

PLATE LXV—PARIS—PONT D'AUTEUIL—MM. BASSOMPIERRE, SUVRIN & VILLERS-DU-TENAGE, ENGINEERS—1865

PLATE LXVI—FRANCE—BRIDGE OVER THE PEDROUSE

PLATE LXVII—LUXEMBURG—PONT ADOLPHE OVER THE PETRUSSE—M. SÉJOURNÉ, ENGINEER—1903

PLATE LXVIII—PISA, ITALY—PONTE SOLFERINO—VINCENZO MICHELI, ARCHITECT—1875

PHOTO BY ALINARI

PLATE LXIX—GENEVA, SWITZERLAND—PONT DE LA COULOUVRENIER OVER THE RHONE—1895
M. CONSTANT BUTTIGAZ, ENGINEER—M. BONVIER, CONSULTING ARCHITECT

PLATE LXX—LAVAUR, FRANCE—BRIDGES OVER THE AGOÛT—BRIDGE IN FOREGROUND BY DE SAGET THE ELDER
BUILT 1791
PHOTO FROM SE'JOURNE'

PLATE LXXI—LAVAUR, FRANCE—PONT DE LAVAUR, SUR L'AGOUT—M. ROBAGLIA, ENGINEER—1884—61.5 METERS SPAN

PHOTO FROM M. PAUL SÉJOURNÉ

PLATE LXXII—ITALY—THE HANNIBAL BRIDGE OVER THE VULTURNE—1870—M. GIUSTINO FIOCCA, ENGINEER

PHOTO FROM M. PAUL SE'JOURNE'

PLATE LXXIII—KEW, ENGLAND—EDWARD VII BRIDGE OVER THE THAMES—1903—SIR JOHN WOLFE BARRY, ENGINEER

PHOTO FROM PUBLISHERS PHOTO SERVICE

PLATE LXXIV—TARN, FRANCE—PONT ANTOINETTE SUR L'AGOUT—M. ROBAGLIA, ENGINEER—1884

PHOTO FROM M. PAUL SÉJOURNÉ

PLATE LXXV—VORAILBERG, AUSTRIA—THE WALDLITOBEL BRIDGE—1884

PHOTO BY M. M. WÜRTHE & SONS, SALSBURG

PLATE LXXVI—ORLEANS, FRANCE—RAILWAY BRIDGE OVER THE LOIRE—BUILT 1906—M. RENARDIER, ENGINEER

PHOTO FROM M. PAUL SE'JOURNE'

PLATE LXXVII—LORRAINE—BRIDGE OVER THE MOSELLE—1905—M. BLUMHARDT, ENGINEER

PLATE LXXVIII—PLAUEN, FREDERIC AUGUST BRIDGE OVER THE SYRA RIVER—1905
SPAN, 90 METERS—C. H. LEIBOLD, ENGINEER

PLATE LXXIX—RONDA, SPAIN—PUENTE NUEVO DEL TAJO DE RONDA—EIGHTEENTH CENTURY
JOSÉ MARTIN ALDEGUELA, ARCHITECT

PLATE LXXX—NEW YORK—HIGH BRIDGE—1842—JOHN H. JERVIS, ENGINEER

PHOTO COPYRIGHTED BY THE DETROIT PUBLISHING CO.

PLATE LXXXI—WASHINGTON, D. C.—CABIN JOHN ARCH—1864—GEN. MEIGS, U. S. A., ENGINEER—SPAN, 220 FEET

PHOTO COPYRIGHTED BY THE DETROIT PUBLISHING CO.

PLATE LXXXII—HARTFORD, CONN.—MEMORIAL BRIDGE OVER THE CONNECTICUT RIVER—1908
A. P. BOLLER, CONSULTING ENGINEER; EDWIN O. GRAVES, CHIEF ENGINEER; E. M. WHEELWRIGHT, ARCHITECT

PHOTO BY HAVEN & CHUDOBA

PLATE LXXXIII

HARRISBURG, PA.—MASONRY VIADUCT OF PENNSYLVANIA RAILROAD OVER THE SUSQUEHANNA RIVER

PHOTO FROM RAU STUDIOS, PHILADELPHIA

PLATE LXXXIV—ELYRIA, OHIO—SOLID MASONRY ARCHES—NEW YORK CENTRAL R. R.—ABOUT 1880

PLATE LXXXV—BEREA, OHIO—MASONRY RAILWAY BRIDGE—NEW YORK CENTRAL R. R.—ABOUT 1880

PLATE LXXXVI—CLEVELAND, OHIO—BRIDGE OVER PARKWAY—C. F. SCHWEINFURTH, ARCHITECT—1902

PLATE LXXXVII—CLEVELAND, OHIO—BRIDGE OVER ROCKEFELLER PARKWAY—C. F. SCHWEINFURTH, ARCHITECT
BUILT 1900

PLATE LXXXVIII—ROME—PONTE VITTORIO EMANUELE II—T. CAPRIATI & ENR. DE'ROSSI, ENGINEERS

PHOTO BY ED. ALINARI

PLATE LXXXIX—ZANESVILLE, OHIO—COVERED TIMBER BRIDGE OVER THE MUSKINGUM & LICKING RIVERS
BUILT 1820—REPLACED 1900

PHOTO BY W. J. W.

IRON AND STEEL ARCH BRIDGES

THE Railroad Age, starting with tremendous impetus in the fourth decade of the nineteenth century, demanded bridges of longer span, designed for heavier loads, than could be built economically of stone masonry or timber, and this demand was met by a vast improvement in the quality of iron and later of steel, as well as in the processes of manufacture, which made possible the production of greatly increased quantities of this material at much lower cost than before.

At first, cast iron was extensively used for bridges of the arch type; then wrought iron chains and later wire cables were provided for bridges of the suspension type, while still later these types were largely superseded by the girder or beam and the articulated truss.

It is unfortunate that this evolution, while progressive from a strictly engineering or utilitarian standpoint, was retrogressive from the viewpoint of architectural merit, this retrogression being due not so much to the type evolution as to the psychology of the times, materialism displacing all higher motives.

The first iron bridge, erected in 1779 over the Severn River in England at Coalbrookdale, had a cast iron arch span of 100 feet.

Possibly the three best examples of the cast metal arch are the old Southwark Bridge in London over the Thames, the great Eads Bridge over the Mississippi River at St. Louis, and the Alexander III Bridge over the Seine at Paris.

The Southwark Bridge, completed in 1819, had a center span of 240 feet and side spans of 210 feet each, constructed of cast iron arches. The design and execution was by John Rennie, the engineer of the Waterloo and New London Bridges.

John Rennie's masterpiece has recently been replaced by a more modern structure, necessitated by the demands of heavier traffic as well as by the settlement of the piers which made the old structure unsafe. This new structure, completed in 1921 from designs by Messrs. Mott, Hay and Anderson of London, has five steel arch spans of 123 to 150 feet clear opening as compared with the three spans of 210 and 240 feet of the old bridge. The plan was developed to conform to the openings in adjacent bridges, resulting in less interference with the river current.

This new Southwark Bridge is a beautiful structure and is a good illustration of what can be accomplished by a combination of steel arches and masonry piers. There is no elaborate ornamentation, the piers being carried above the roadway level to form a series of simple pylons.

Sir Ernest George, A. R. A., collaborated with the engineers in the design of the masonry piers and abutments. (Plates XC & XCI.)

The second bridge to be built over the Thames at London was the Westminster Bridge, completed in 1750 as a masonry structure of thirteen arches, designed by a French engineer, Charles Labelye. It was of the view of the city from this bridge that Wordsworth wrote, "Earth has not anything to show more fair." Labelye's Bridge was characterized by unusually high parapets, a feature that a French writer (Parisian) declared was intended to prevent the Londoners from committing suicide. Possibly his opinion of the view did not agree with that of Wordsworth.

The old Westminster Bridge lasted a little better than a century, being replaced by the existing steel structure in 1862. Its failure was due to the gradual undermining of its foundations by the river, a fate that also befell the Blackfriars Bridge (the third to be built across the Thames, in 1769, by Robert Mylne). And now the river has at last (1926) conquered Rennie's Waterloo bridge. (Plate XCII.)

⸎ ⸎ ⸎

The Blackfriars Bridge was rebuilt in 1865, under the direction of Joseph Cubitt, engineer, and was widened in 1908 by Sir Benjamin Baker.

⸎ ⸎ ⸎

At Constantine, Algeria, there is a fine cast iron arch bridge, completed by the French in 1865 and bearing the inscription of Napoleon III. The architect in charge was M. Martin. (Plate XCIII.)

⸎ ⸎ ⸎

The Alexandre III Bridge at Paris, built also with cast steel ribs, in 1899, has already been described. (Page 111.)

⸎ ⸎ ⸎

The famous Eads Bridge at St. Louis was built in the years 1868 to 1874 by James B.

Eads, one of America's most noted engineers. The arch ribs are of cast steel and have a clear span of 520 feet with a rise of 47 feet for the central arch and a clear span of 502 feet for the flanking spans. The construction of this bridge was considered to be a great engineering achievement in its day and it has safely carried the greatly increased loads of modern highway and railroad traffic. Its graceful arches are a pleasing contrast to the more modern trusses of its neighbors.

"Although some of its details have been altered and strengthened, the main frame of braced arch tubes is still intact as originally constructed and is carrying present day traffic in volume and weight far beyond the designs and expectations of its builders. This unusual record is a fine tribute to the work and personality of James B. Eads.* About 600,000 passenger and freight cars and over 50,000 locomotives cross the bridge each year. The bridge cost about $7,000,000." (C. E. Smith, before the American Railway Bridge and Building Association, 1924.) (Plate XCIV.)

---

*Mr. J. B. Eads, the eminent American engineer who conceived and executed this noble project, against great odds, made the following statement in the course of an address delivered in 1871. The sentiment expressed therein seems to be worthy of repetition here. He was speaking of the Missouri River.

"My experience of this current has taught me that eternal vigilance is the price of safety, and constant watchfulness is one of the first requisites to insure success, almost as much as knowledge and experience. To the superficial observer, this stream seems to override old-established theories, and to set at naught the apparently best devised schemes of science. But yet there moves no grain of sand through its devious channel, in its course to the sea, that is not governed by laws more fixed than any that were known to the code of the Medes and Persians. No giant tree, standing on its banks, bows its stately head beneath these dark waters, except in obedience to laws which have been created in the goodness and wisdom of Our Heavenly Father, to govern the conditions of matter at rest and in motion."

The Whipple Truss

Cast iron was extensively used in the early part of the nineteenth century, in America, for the compression members of truss bridges. Hundreds of structures of the arched truss or "Bowstring" type, with the upper chord curved in form and made up of cast iron segments, while the lower and intermediate members were of wrought iron, are still in use. This type of arch was known as the Whipple Truss, after its inventor, Squire Whipple, of Utica, New York, to whom belongs the honor of having been the first engineer correctly to analyze the stresses in the articulated truss, in his book on bridge building published in 1847. For centuries, engineers and architects had been building bridges without much mathematical knowledge of the stresses involved, but relying simply upon past experience and good judgment in proportioning the various members composing the structure. These old Whipple arch bridges are better looking than many more modern types of metal bridges, but are being rapidly displaced by structures designed for heavier loads. Bowstring trusses of this type have been built up to 187 feet span. (Plate XCV.)

During the nineteenth century, material improvements were made in the processes of manufacturing wrought iron, and in the last quarter of that century wrought iron began to be displaced by steel. These improvements rendered possible the economical use of wrought iron and steel for bridge construction of all types, the beam or girder type, the cantilever type, the arch, the truss and even the suspension type. This strong and inexpensive material made possible the construction of much larger spans than heretofore. In the case of the arch type, spans have constantly increased in length, culminating in such a structure as the Hell Gate Arch at New York with its single span of nearly a thousand feet.

Some of these great modern steel arches are structures of great beauty, as the Washington Bridge at New York, the Garabit Viaduct in France, the bridge over the Rhine at Bonn, Germany, the Upper Steel Arch at Niagara Falls, and a bridge over the Aar at Berne, Switzerland. Some more modest structures of the steel arch type are also worthy of note, many by reason of the artistic treatment of the combination of masonry and steel, as exemplified by the Charles River Bridge at Boston, and by some bridges on the Nickel Plate Railway at Cleveland, as illustrated in the plates.

The Washington Bridge at New York, over the Harlem River, was completed in 1889. This beautiful structure consists of twin arch spans 508 feet 9 inches in length each, and having a rise of 83 feet 4 inches. The arch ribs are segmental plate girders, supporting numerous vertical posts which carry the roadway floor. The designer was Wm. R. Hutton, chief engineer, with E. H. Kendall as consulting architect. The designer of this bridge obtained a pleasing symmetrical design in spite of a very unsymmetrical profile. (Plate XCVI.)

The Garabit Viaduct over the Truyere, France, built in 1884, carries a single track railroad over a deep and rocky gorge. The graceful parabolic arch is a latticed truss, deeper in the center than at the ends, and has a span of 166 meters with a rise of 52 meters. The arch rib carries but two posts and two more are carried by the abutments. These posts have a pronounced batter and are latticed like the arch ribs, as are also the trusses. The effect is that of extreme simplicity and harmony in steel. The design is due to M. Eiffel. (Plate XCVII.)

⸎ ⸎ ⸎

The Rhine Bridge at Bonn consists of a single long and high steel arch flanked by shorter low arches. This bridge was completed in 1897. The main span is 188 meters in length, between piers, while the side spans are each 96 meters long. The main span is a trussed steel arch deeper at the ends than in the center, segmental in curvature, and carrying a roadway most of which is below the arch and suspended therefrom. The flanking arches are of the deck type. Features of the Bonn Bridge are the beautifully proportioned piers, surmounted by Romanesque towers at the ends of the main span and the cast iron ornamental portals and railings.

Bruno Möhring, of Berlin, was consulting architect for this project. (Plate XCVIII.)

⸎ ⸎ ⸎

A steel arched highway Bridge at Berne, Switzerland, over the River Aar, completed in 1898, is similar in conception to the Garabit Viaduct with this difference, that the latticed arch ribs are deepest at the springing, and decrease in thickness to a comparatively shallow thickness at the crown, just the reverse of the Garabit Bridge. The arch ribs support eight high, tapered, latticed columns, which carry latticed trusses. The main arch is 114.86 meters span by 31½ meters rise. A comparison

of this design with that of the Niagara arch is very much in its favor for architectural merit, although doubtless this type is somewhat less economical of material. The credit for the design of this very handsome bridge belongs to A. and H. Bonstetten, engineers, and B. H. Von Fischer, consulting architect. (Plate XCIX.)

⸎ ⸎ ⸎

At Rüdesheim, Germany, there is a railway bridge over the Rhine that comprises two steel arches flanked by simple steel trusses, so arranged that they seem to fit the regimen of the stream unusually well. (Plate C.)

⸎ ⸎ ⸎

The Upper Steel Arch at Niagara Falls, officially called the Niagara Falls and Clifton Bridge, completed in 1898, carries a highway over the raging torrent of the Niagara gorge just below the great falls, with a single span of 840 feet and a rise of 137 feet. The arch is parabolic in curvature and the main span is flanked on each end with a shorter inverted parabolic arched truss. The main arch rib is hinged at the ends only, increasing in depth from the ends to the center, and is trussed, carrying vertical posts stiffened by horizontal braces. The engineer in charge was Mr. L. L. Buck. (Plate CII.)

⸎ ⸎ ⸎

The great steel arch bridge of the New York Connecting Railway, carrying its double track over Long Island Sound at Little Hell Gate, was completed in 1916, after designs by Gustav Lindenthal. This magnificent structure comprises a single steel arch of 977½ feet span, flanked by a high trestle on each side, from which it is separated by massive masonry towers serving as the abutments of the arch span. The main arch rises to a height of nearly 300 feet above the river. The intrados is parabolic in curvature while the extrados curve is reversed near the abutments, where the depth between the intradosal and extradosal curves becomes greatest. An idea of the magnitude of this structure may be obtained from the quantities of material required, about 210,000 tons of steel and 108,000 yards of masonry being used. (Plate CIII.)

✦ ✦ ✦

The Cambridge Bridge at Boston, Massachusetts, completed in 1908, is one of the finest steel arch bridges in the world. The present structure replaces the old West Boston Bridge, which Longfellow immortalized in "The Bridge," and consists of eleven spans of steel plate arches abutting against massive granite piers. The center or channel span of 188½ feet is flanked by large piers carrying ornamental stone towers. The engineer-in-chief was William Jackson and Edmund Wheelwright was consulting architect. The cost was about two and one-half million dollars. (Plate CIV.)

✦ ✦ ✦

Many small steel arch bridges of merit have been built, most of them, of course, with no attempt at architectural treatment. Among those that show architectural study are some street crossings of the Nickel Plate Railroad in East Cleveland, Ohio, designed by the late A. J. Himes. When compared with the customary designs of such structures, these bridges deserve commendation. (Plate CV.)

Two graceful steel arch bridges, one in Riverside Cemetery, Cleveland, and the other near Cleveland, constructed in the early nineties, are the work of the late Frank C. Osborn of that city. (Plate CVI.)

✦ ✦ ✦

A German bridge over the Rhine at Worms, completed in 1901 by the engineers Schneider and Frintzen, and consisting of three steel arches, at the ends of which have been erected elaborate portal towers, has a distinctive character. (Plate CVII.)

✦ ✦ ✦

The new bridge at Fortieth Street, Pittsburgh, known as the Washington Crossing Bridge, consists of three steel arch spans, supported by well-proportioned concrete piers.

The Sixteenth Street Bridge at Pittsburgh, recently completed, comprises three trussed steel arches of the overhead type and here again the charm of the structure is due largely to the design of the piers and abutments.

Mr. V. R. Covell is the engineer in charge of these Pittsburgh bridges and Messrs. Warren & Wetmore were the architects for the Sixteenth Street Bridge and Benno Janssen for the Fortieth Street Bridge. (Plates CVIII & CIX.)

PLATE XC—LONDON—THE NEW SOUTHWARK BRIDGE—COMPLETED 1921—MOTT, HAY & ANDERSON, ENGINEERS
SIR ERNEST GEORGE, ARCHITECT
PHOTO BY GENERAL PHOTOGRAPHIC AGENCY, LONDON

PLATE XCI—LONDON—NEW SOUTHWARK BRIDGE OVER THE THAMES—1921—MOTT, HAY & ANDERSON, ENGINEERS
SIR ERNEST GEORGE, ARCHITECT

PHOTO FROM GENERAL PHOTOGRAPHIC AGENCY, LONDON

PLATE XCII—LONDON—WESTMINSTER BRIDGE OVER THE RIVER THAMES—1862

PHOTO FROM GENERAL PHOTOGRAPHIC AGENCY, LONDON

PLATE XCIII—CONSTANTINE, ALGERIA—EL KANTARA BRIDGE—M. MARTIN, ARCHITECT—1865

COPYRIGHT BY THE PUBLISHERS PHOTO SERVICE

PLATE XCIV—ST. LOUIS, MO.—THE EADS BRIDGE OVER THE MISSISSIPPI RIVER—1874—JAS. B. EADS, ENGINEER

PHOTO FROM DETROIT PUBLISHING CO.

PLATE XCV—TYPICAL "BOWSTRING" ARCH—WHIPPLE TYPE—EASTERN UNITED STATES—1850

PHOTO BY W. J. W.

PLATE XCVI—NEW YORK—WASHINGTON BRIDGE OVER THE HARLEM RIVER—1889—SPANS 508 FEET 9 INCHES EACH
WM. R. HUTTON, CHIEF ENGINEER. E. H. KENDELL, CONSULTING ARCHITECT
PHOTO COPYRIGHTED BY THE DETROIT PUBLISHING CO.

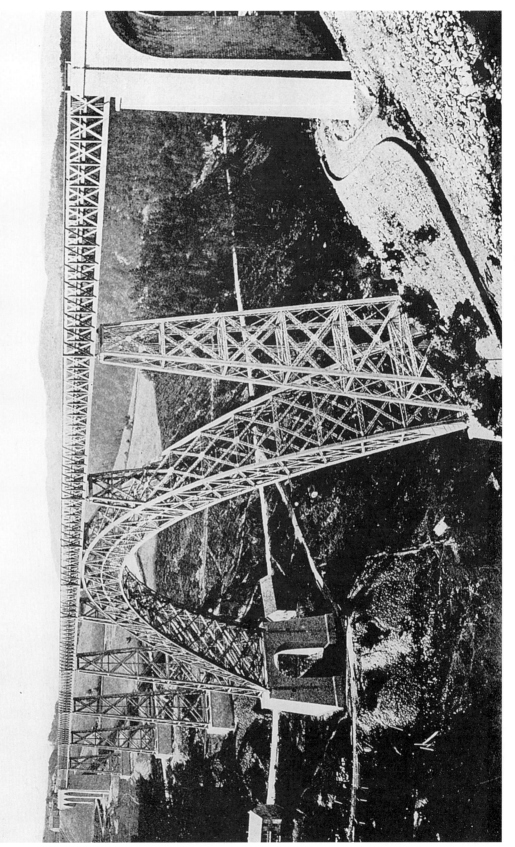

PLATE XCVII—FRANCE—GARABIT VIADUCT—M. EIFFEL, ENGINEER—1884

PLATE XCVIII—BONN, GERMANY—STEEL ARCH BRIDGE OVER THE RHINE—COMPLETED 1897
BRUNO MÖHRING, BERLIN, CONSULTING ARCHITECT

PLATE XCIX—BERNE, SWITZERLAND—BRIDGE OVER THE AAR—1898—A. & H. VON BONSTETTEN, ENGINEERS
B. H. VON FISCHER, ARCHITECT

PLATE C—RÜDESHEIM, GERMANY—RAILWAY BRIDGE OVER THE RHINE

PHOTO FROM MASCHINENFABRIK AUGSBURG-NÜRNBERG A. G.

PLATE CI—COLOGNE, GERMANY—RAILWAY AND HIGHWAY BRIDGE OVER THE RHINE—MODERN

PHOTO BY GEUS, KOLN.   DESIGNED BY MASCHINENFABRIK AUGSBERG-NÜRNBERG A. G.

PLATE CII—NIAGARA FALLS, N. Y.—NIAGARA-CLIFTON BRIDGE—L. L. BUCK, ENGINEER—1898

PHOTO BY W. J. W.

PLATE CIII—NEW YORK, N. Y.—HELL GATE BRIDGE—1916—GUSTAV LINDENTHAL, ENGINEER

PHOTO COPYRIGHTED BY THE DETROIT PUBLISHING CO.

PLATE CIV—BOSTON, MASS.—THE LONGFELLOW BRIDGE OVER THE CHARLES RIVER—1908
WILLIAM JACKSON, CHIEF ENGINEER.   EDMUND WHEELWRIGHT, CONSULTING ARCHITECT

PLATE CIV-B—DETAIL—LONGFELLOW BRIDGE   DETAIL—LONGFELLOW BRIDGE

PLATE CV—EAST CLEVELAND, OHIO—STREET CROSSING OF N. Y. C. & ST. L. RY.—A. J. HIMES, ENGINEER

PLATE CVI—CLEVELAND, OHIO—HIGHWAY BRIDGE IN RIVERSIDE CEMETERY—ABOUT 1896
FRANK C. OSBORN, ENGINEER

PLATE CVI-B—CHAGRIN FALLS, OHIO—STEEL ARCH BRIDGE DESIGNED BY FRANK C. OSBORN

PLATE CVII—WORMS, GERMANY—HIGHWAY BRIDGE OVER THE RHINE—1901—ENGINEERS, HN. SCHNEIDER & FRINTZEN

PHOTO FROM MASCHINENFABRIK AUGSBERG-NÜRNBERG A. G.

PLATE CVIII—PITTSBURGH, PA.—FORTIETH STREET BRIDGE OVER THE ALLEGHENY RIVER—COMPLETED 1924
V. R. COVELL, CHIEF ENGINEER. BENNO JANSSEN, ARCHITECT

PLATE CIX—PITTSBURGH, PA.—SIXTEENTH STREET BRIDGE OVER THE ALLEGHENY RIVER—COMPLETED 1923
V. R. COVELL, CHIEF ENGINEER. WARREN & WETMORE, ARCHITECTS

MODERN SUSPENSION BRIDGES

THE Suspension Bridge is the natural reverse of the arched type, the arch turned upside down, so to speak, and is one of the earliest types, having been used extensively by Asiatic peoples since prehistoric times. Until quite recently, however, the type was undeveloped, due primarily to the lack of proper materials for heavy construction. During the last century it has been highly developed by Telford in England, Ellet and Roebling in the United States, and others. Some of these structures are beautiful and worthy to be classed among our great monumental bridges, notably the three incomparable spans over the East River at New York, and the recently completed Philadelphia-Camden Bridge.

As the suspension type of bridge necessarily utilizes more perishable materials in its construction as compared to the masonry arch, no ancient structures of this type have come down to us intact. There exist in many places, however, structures that have been maintained without change of design or construction for many centuries. Among these are the suspension bridges of Asia, as an illustration of which we have selected a bridge located in northern Sze-Chuan, China. This bridge is constructed of cables of woven bamboo, supported on and anchored to heavy masonry piers, which carry timber and stucco houses. (Plate VII.)

At Newburyport, Massachusetts, there is an old suspension bridge, built in 1810, and still in use, although similar to many other bridges that have outlived their usefulness and been replaced by stronger, and often uglier, types. This bridge was built by one John Templeton, and has a span of 244 feet. The cables or suspenders are made up of chains. It has just recently been repaired and rebuilt by Prof. George W. Swain, after more than a century of service. (Plate CX.)

One of the most famous suspension bridges in the world is the Menai Straits Bridge in Wales, built by Telford and completed in 1826 after seven years' work. This was at that time the largest suspension bridge yet built, having a main span of 579 feet with approaches of high massive masonry arches. The length over all is 1710 feet and there are two driveways 12 feet wide each and one walk 4 feet wide. (Plate CXI.)

Suspension Bridges at Budapest

Among European bridges notable for their beauty are two suspension bridges at Budapest over the Danube. The more recent bridge of Budapest is known as the Elizabeth Bridge and was completed in 1905 after designs by A. Czechelius, with M. Nagy as collaborating architect. The main span is 290 meters in length and the length over all 920 meters. Massive masonry pylons over the anchorages form the principal architectural feature. The older and more beautiful structure, known as the Kettenbrücke, has a span of 203 meters and was completed in 1849 after plans by W. T. Tierney Clarke. It has well-proportioned masonry towers and abutments, the latter with carved lions ornamenting the end posts.

While not the equal of some of our recent American bridges in magnitude of span, there can be no doubt of the superior architectural value of these two structures. (Plates CXII & CXIII.)

The practical development of the suspension bridge to suit modern requirements has taken place in America, and many of the American bridges possess also aesthetic merit, inherent in the natural gracefulness of the type, when well designed. Some of the earlier and more spectacular structures, such as the bridges over the Niagara gorge, have disappeared, and have been replaced by more rigid types which are doubtless more utilitarian, but unfortunately somewhat less pleasing to the eye.

The grandfather of this type in the United States is the old bridge over the Ohio River at Wheeling, West Virginia, constructed by Col. Ellet in 1846 to 1849, as a link in the National Highway from Washington to the West. It has a span of 1010 feet. During a storm in 1854, the stiffening trusses were wrecked, a lesson that led to a careful study of this essential part of the design which made possible later the great and successful bridges at New York. This bridge was reconstructed in 1862 by Col. John A. Roebling and is still in service, a delight to look upon. Col. Roebling later completed a similar bridge, having a span of 1260 feet, across the Niagara

River below the falls. This structure was rebuilt, with heavier cables, in 1889, and still later was replaced with a steel arch. This latter became a famous bridge, due largely to its spectacular location at the greatest honeymoon resort in North America.

New York—Brooklyn Bridge

Col. Roebling then undertook the construction, as engineer-contractor, of the Brooklyn Bridge over the East River at New York, which was completed, against great odds, financial as well as engineering, in 1883. This huge structure, justly celebrated as one of the greatest achievements of engineering, also possesses artistic merit of a high degree. Possibly its designers had little intention of erecting a work of art, but of the result there can be no doubt. No sculpture, no ornamentation of any kind is used, or needed. Its simple and dignified design is all that is necessary. Mr. Roebling made a report to the president and directors of the Bridge Company in 1867, which closed with these words: "The contemplated work, when constructed in accordance with my designs, will not only be the greatest bridge in existence, but it will be the great engineering work of this continent and of the age.

"Its most conspicuous features—the great towers—will serve as landmarks to the adjoining cities, and they will be entitled to be ranked as national monuments. As a great work of art, and as a successful specimen of advanced bridge engineering, this structure will forever testify to the energy, enterprise and wealth of that community which shall secure its erection." Surely this great engineer possessed the imagination of a genius, as well as the feeling of the artist. To quote again from his writings, "Honesty of design and execution, next to knowledge and experience, most surely guarantees professional reputation." Most excellent advice to both engineers and architects! Col. Roebling, however, did not live to see the completion of this great work. While personally laying out the towers, he received injuries which caused his death in July, 1867. The work was completed by his gifted son, Col. Washington Roebling. This noble structure has a main span of 1595 feet 6 inches, and a clear height above the water of 135 feet, allowing ocean-going vessels to pass underneath. Its decks accommodate two elevated railway tracks, two surface traction tracks, two roadways and one walkway. The cost was about sixteen million dollars. (Plate CXIV.)

New York—Williamsburg and Manhattan Bridges

Since the building of the Brooklyn Bridge, two other suspension bridges have been built over the East River at New York, known as the Williamsburg Bridge, completed in 1903, and the Manhattan Bridge, completed in 1909.

The former has very little to commend from an architectural viewpoint. The staunch stone towers of the Brooklyn Bridge are paralleled by awkward-looking towers of steel. In the design of the Manhattan Bridge, however, we witness a return to pleasing proportions, made possible by a radical change in the principles of construction, consisting in securing the cables at the tops of the towers, thus doing away with the clumsy saddles, and

hinging the tower itself at its base to allow it to rock to and fro with the variations in length and sag of the cables. This change permitted the use of a comparatively slender tower of steel of pleasing form and proportion.

No consulting architect was employed on the general design of the Williamsburg Bridge.

The Manhattan Bridge has a span of 1470 feet, while the span of the Williamsburg Bridge is 1600 feet, exceeded only by the Philadelphia-Camden Bridge recently completed. Carere and Hastings were consulting architects on the Manhattan Bridge, collaborating with the engineers of the Department of Plant and Structures of the City of New York. (Plates CXV & CXVI.)

Engineering of New York Bridges*

The construction of the great East River Bridges at New York was made possible by the development of modern methods and materials of engineering. Perhaps the most important development was that of the pneumatic caisson, by means of which foundations

---

*Physical data regarding New York East River Bridges:
Brooklyn Bridge: Length over all, 7811 ft. 6 in. River span, 1595 ft. 6 in. Height of towers, 272 ft. Cables, 15¾ in. diameter. Weight of metal, 21,920 tons. Masonry in piers, 85,160 cu. yds. Capacity, two elevated railway tracks, two surface railway tracks, two roadways, 16 ft. 9 in. wide, and one footwalk 15 ft. 7 in. wide.
Williamsburg Bridge: Length over all, 8908 ft. River span, 1600 ft. Height of towers, 333 ft. Diameter of cables, 18.625 in. Weight of metal, 45,285 tons. Masonry, 158,300 cu. yds. Total cost, $14,181,560.00. Capacity, six tracks, two roadways, 19 ft. 11 in. each, and two foot walks, 17 ft. 8 in.
Manhattan Bridge: Length over all, 8325 ft. Length of river span, 1470 ft. Height of towers, 322 ft. 6 in. Diameter of cables, 21¼ in. Weight of metal, 59,450 tons. Masonry, 308,000 cu. yds. total. Capacity, eight tracks, one roadway, 35 ft. wide, two walks, 13 ft. 7 in. wide. Cost $14,000,000.00.
Queensboro Bridge: Length over all, 7450 ft. Longest spans, 1182 ft. Height, 323 ft. Weight of steel, 73,800 tons. Masonry, 106,000 cu. yds. Cost, $13,500,000.00. Completed in 1909.

in water could be carried to much greater depths than was before possible.

The pneumatic caisson is an adaptation of the diving bell, consisting of a chamber open at the bottom only, and supplied with compressed air, the pressure being varied to compensate the exterior water pressure. Workmen operating in compressed air (called sand-hogs) can work only in short shifts.

The pneumatic caisson was used in the construction of the Forth Bridge in Scotland, the Eads Bridge at St. Louis, which was its first notable application in America, and for all of the East River Bridges.

Another important factor was the improvement of steel wire, making available strands of much stronger material than it had heretofore been possible to obtain, and allowing the construction of suspension bridges of larger span.

Coincident with these developments was a much more accurate knowledge, on the part of engineers, of the properties of materials, and of the stresses and strains involved in bridge structures, a knowledge that came from the establishment of engineering colleges and from testing laboratories.

Philadelphia-Camden Bridge

The Philadelphia-Camden Suspension Bridge,* the largest and newest of the type, was completed in 1926 after more than a hun-

---

*Physical data regarding Philadelphia-Camden Bridge: Total length, including approaches, 9570 ft. Length of main span, 1750 ft. Width of bridge, 128 ft. Width of roadway, 57 ft. Height of towers above water, 380 ft. Clearance of bridge above mean high water, 135 ft. Deepest foundation below mean high water, 105 ft. Diameter of cables, 30 in. Total length of wire used, 25,100 miles. Granite masonry, 25,200 cu. yds. Concrete masonry, 289,800 cu. yds. Structural steel, 61,700 tons.

dred years' agitation for a bridge at this site, at a cost of about twenty-five million dollars, exclusive of real estate. It is the only bridge crossing the Delaware River at Philadelphia. The engineers in charge were Ralph Modjeski, George S. Webster and Lawrence A. Ball, with Paul E. Cret as architect and Clement E. Chase as resident engineer. This huge structure carries a 57-foot wide roadway, four railway tracks and two footwalks. (Plates CXVII & CXVIII.)

' ' '

Two charming suspension bridges have recently been built which illustrate clearly the architectural advantages inherent in this type. These are the new bridge over the Rhine at Cologne, completed in 1915, and the Seventh Street Bridge at Pittsburgh over the Allegheny River, completed in 1926. These two structures are quite similar in design. The Cologne bridge has a center span of 184.4 meters, flanked by two side spans of 92.2 meters each. (Plate CXIX).

Pittsburgh—Seventh Avenue Bridge

The bridge over the Allegheny River on Seventh Avenue, Pittsburgh, a beautiful structure, recently completed, is but one of many bridges planned to cross the Allegheny and Monongahela Rivers at Pittsburgh. They will replace older structures that fail to meet navigation requirements. This structure is of the self-anchored suspension type. The main span is about 442 feet long and the side spans 221 feet long, while the roadway is 37½ feet wide between curbs, with a sidewalk on each side. The similarity of this design to that employed for the new suspension bridge across the Rhine at Cologne, and, with the exception of the use of metal towers instead of masonry, to those at Budapest, is notable. These Pittsburgh bridges are being constructed by Allegheny County, of which V. R. Covell is chief engineer of bridges, and the program comprises some forty-three bridges to be constructed during a period of ten years, and entailing an expenditure of about $23,000,000. (Plate CXX.)

The peculiar charm of the suspension bridge is due largely to the fact that the system of stresses and strains involved is the most simple possible, and every main member of the structure expresses strongly the part that it plays in the system.

PLATE CX—NEWBURYPORT, MASS.—OLD CHAIN SUSPENSION BRIDGE—1810—JOHN TEMPLETON, BUILDER
PHOTO COPYRIGHTED BY THE DETROIT PUBLISHING CO.

PLATE CXI—MENAI STRAIT, WALES—TELFORD'S SUSPENSION BRIDGE—1826

PLATE CXII—BUDAPEST, HUNGARY—KETTENBRÜCKE—1849—W. T. TIERNEY CLARKE, ENGINEER
PHOTO BY ERDÉLYI, BUDAPEST

PLATE CXIII—BUDAPEST, HUNGARY—ELIZABETH BRIDGE—A. CZECHELIUS, ENGINEER.   M. NAGY, ARCHITECT
COMPLETED 1905
PHOTO BY ERDÉLYI, BUDAPEST

PLATE CXIV—NEW YORK—BROOKLYN BRIDGE—1883—COL. JOHN A. ROEBLING, ENGINEER

PHOTO FROM DEPARTMENT OF PLANT AND STRUCTURES, NEW YORK

PLATE CXV—NEW YORK—WILLIAMSBURG BRIDGE OVER THE EAST RIVER

PLATE CXVI—NEW YORK—MANHATTAN BRIDGE OVER THE EAST RIVER—1909—DEPARTMENT OF PLANT & STRUCTURES OF THE CITY OF NEW YORK, ENGINEERS. CARRERE & HASTINGS, CONSULTING ARCHITECTS

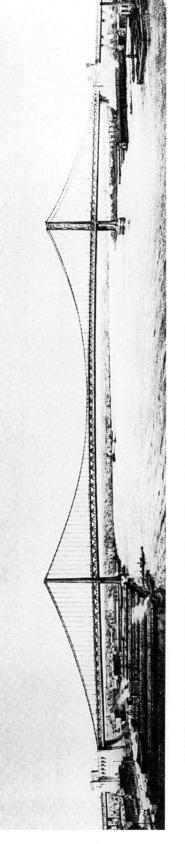

PLATE CXVII—PHILADELPHIA-CAMDEN BRIDGE OVER THE DELAWARE RIVER—1926—RALPH MODJESKI, CHIEF ENGINEER
PAUL E. CRET, ARCHITECT

PLATE CXVIII—PHILADELPHIA-CAMDEN BRIDGE—DETAIL OF ANCHOR PIER—1926
RALPH MODJESKI, CHIEF ENGINEER; PAUL E. CRET, ARCHITECT

PLATE CXIX—COLOGNE, GERMANY—SUSPENSION BRIDGE OVER THE RHINE—1915—W. DIETZ, ENGINEER

PLATE CXX—PITTSBURGH, PA.—SEVENTH AVENUE BRIDGE OVER ALLEGHENY RIVER—MAIN SPAN 442 FEET—1926
V. R. COVELL, CHIEF ENGINEER

MODERN CANTILEVER BRIDGES

THE only competitor, from an engineering standpoint, of the suspension type of bridge when used for long spans, is the cantilever type, and this is generally conceded to excel all other types in its innate ugliness. Its complicated system of trussing is utterly unintelligible to the layman, and being unintelligible, is necessarily offensive. Even when of great and noble proportions, as the huge Forth Bridge in Scotland, or the Quebec Bridge in Canada, or the Queensboro Bridge in New York, it cannot give to the eye that pleasure which is furnished by the arch and the suspension types. On the other hand, the cantilever type furnishes a more rigid structure than the suspension type and so is better adapted to carry heavy, concentrated loads.

Although these great cantilever bridges are all of recent construction, the cantilever type is not recent, as the principle has been used since the earliest times. These early bridges, however, are primitive and almost invariably make use of a series of cantilevered beams such as shown by the picture of an old bridge at Bhutan in Thibet, consisting of cantilevered wooden beams, weighted down at the shore or pier end by stone masonry. (Plate II.)

One of the most important structures of this type in America is the Queensboro Bridge over the East River at New York, completed in 1909, formerly known as the Blackwells Island Bridge. (See page 174 for physical data.)

The Queensboro Bridge was designed by the engineers of the Department of Plant and Structures, with Henry F. Hornbostel as consulting architect. (Plate CXXI.)

Bridge over the Firth of Forth

Of all the great cantilever bridges, this bridge is doubtless the most famous. It is the work of Sir John Fowler and Sir Benjamin Baker and consists of three huge cantilevers, 1700 feet span and 336 feet in height. The lower chords of the cantilevers are curved and brought close to the water at the springing line, and this fact, together with the comparatively short length of the suspended span, 350 feet, gives the general effect of two huge arches and two half arches.

The simplicity of the truss system, obtained by the use of as few members as practicable, and those of large size, also contributes to the peculiar appeal of this structure. Unfortunately, engineers are agreed that this does not result in the maximum economy of material and the old question then arises—Is it allowable for the engineer to depart from the requirements of absolute economy in the design of a bridge, and adopt a more pleasing outline at somewhat greater cost? The right and duty of an architect so to do in the case of a monumental building is not questioned. Why should not the engineer be allowed the same privilege, or rather, be taught the same duty? This bridge carries a double track railway and was completed in 1883. (Plate CXXII.)

A design of cantilever bridge extensively used consists of one or more simple truss spans having the ends cantilevered out beyond the piers and supporting shorter and shallower suspended spans. Typical of this type is the bridge over the Hudson River at Poughkeepsie, New York, the Queensboro Bridge over the East River at New York and the bridge over the Mississippi River at Thebes, Illinois.

One of the most famous bridges in the world, and holding the record clear span of 1800 feet, is the Quebec Bridge over the St. Lawrence River, located about nine miles above Quebec, Canada, where the river is comparatively narrow, but more than 200 feet deep. This great structure carries two railroad tracks over the river at a clearance for boats of 150 feet and was completed in 1912 after the failure of one structure, which collapsed during erection. This accident occurred on August 29, 1907, causing the loss of seventy-four workmen. The ancient saying that "the bridge demands a life" was more than exemplified in this structure, which demanded many. The design of the structure as finally built was made by Phelps Johnson and G. H. Duggan, of the St. Lawrence Bridge Company, acting with an advisory board of five engineers, of which Ralph Modjeski was chairman. (Plate CXXIII.)

The bridge at Thebes, Illinois, built in 1905, after designs by Alfred Noble and Ralph Modjeski, both eminent American engineers, has a length of 2597 feet over all, and comprises one span of about 790 feet and two of 621 feet. The trusses are so nearly uniform in depth that they give the appearance of continuous trusses, a type of bridge not much different in appearance. (Plate CXXIV.)

Simple Steel Trusses and Girders

The homely and economical simple truss and girder bridges, built by the hundreds to carry the railroads which have covered the face of the land with a network of iron paths during the past century, over river and valley obstructing their way, have too often been the subject of unmerited abuse. Ugly most of them are, without question, and yet not all. Some are beautiful in their simple lines, and others have a distinct charm, especially when combined with masonry abutments and piers of good outline and proportion.

The European truss bridge is usually of the so-called multiple intersection type, as contrasted to the typical American practice of single members, forming triangles and as few in number as practicable. Doubtless the multiple system is more pleasing to the eye; it is more complete and more logical to the untechnical mind.

As typical examples of good American and European practice in the design of bridges of simple trusses and girders, the following structures have been selected for illustration:

Railroad Bridge over Street, London. (Plate CXXV.)

Bridge over the Hudson at Castleton, N. Y. (Plate CXXVI.)

Bridge over the Susquehanna River at Havre de Grace, Maryland. (Plate CXXVII.)

Bridge over the Rhine at Mayence, Germany. (Plate CXXVIII.)

Steel Railway Bridge over the Rhine at Cologne, Germany. (Plate CXXIX.)

Steel girder Railway Bridge at Cleveland, Ohio. (Plate CXXXI.)

PLATE CXXI—NEW YORK—QUEENSBORO BRIDGE OVER THE EAST RIVER—1909—DESIGNED BY THE DEPARTMENT OF
PLANT & STRUCTURES, CITY OF NEW YORK—HENRY F. HORNBOSTEL, CONSULTING ARCHITECT

PLATE CXXII—SCOTLAND—THE FORTH BRIDGE—1883—SIR JOHN FOWLER AND SIR BENJ. BAKER, ENGINEERS
PHOTO COPYRIGHT BY THE PUBLISHERS PHOTO SERVICE

PLATE CXXIII—QUEBEC, CANADA—BRIDGE OVER THE ST. LAWRENCE—1917—RALPH MODJESKI, CHIEF ENGINEER

PLATE CXXIV—THEBES, ILL.—BRIDGE OVER THE MISSISSIPPI RIVER—COMPLETED 1905—ALFRED NOBLE AND RALPH MODJESKI, ENGINEERS

PHOTO BY CRISTIE, CHICAGO

PLATE CXXV—LONDON—RAILROAD BRIDGE OVER STREET—ST. PAUL'S IN BACKGROUND

PHOTO FROM GENERAL PHOTOGRAPHIC AGENCY, LONDON

PLATE CXXVI—CASTLETON, N. Y.—BRIDGE CARRYING NEW YORK CENTRAL R. R. OVER THE HUDSON RIVER
H. T. WELTY, BRIDGE ENGINEER, N. Y. C. R. R.—1926

PHOTO FROM H. G. BARTLETT, ALBANY, N. Y.

PLATE CXXVII—HAVRE DE GRACE, MD.—BALTIMORE & OHIO R. R. BRIDGE OVER SUSQUEHANNA RIVER

PLATE CXXVIII—MAYENCE, GERMANY—THE NEW BRIDGE OVER THE RHINE

PLATE CXXIX—COLOGNE, GERMANY—RAILWAY BRIDGE OVER THE RHINE—1859—STATUE OF WILLIAM IV,
BY BLASER, AND OF WILLIAM II, BY DRAKE

PLATE CXXX—COBLENZ, GERMANY—BRIDGE OVER THE RHINE

PLATE CXXXI—CLEVELAND, OHIO—RAILROAD BRIDGE OVER EAST 30TH STREET—BUILT 1918
WILBUR J. WATSON, ENGINEER

MODERN CONCRETE BRIDGES

THE invention of reinforced concrete has placed in the hands of modern bridge engineers a new material in which to work, a material that, to many intents and purposes, is stone masonry, but stone masonry that has the property of offering great resistance to tensile stresses, by virtue of the steel embedded within, which is protected by the surrounding concrete from corrosion.

Furthermore, this material is plastic and can be cast into any desired form, at less expense than similar forms can be cut out of the natural stone. It is evident, therefore, that the new material offers to the bridge engineer and to the architect collaborating in bridge design, a great opportunity. That the engineers and architects have not been oblivious to the opportunity is evidenced by many beautiful structures built of this material in the last two decades, especially those located in the United States, which are, as a rule, more pleasing than the much lighter and apparently attenuated forms generally used abroad.

It was only two decades ago that the chief engineer of one of the greatest American railroad systems was quoted as saying that concrete would not be used by that company, because he did not believe, and no one could make him believe, that man could make as good a building stone as that made by the Creator. But concrete is now a standard building material of that great railroad system as of most others in the construction of bridges for which cut stone was formerly used. Unquestionably, concrete constructions do not possess the same charm as well designed and executed cut stone masonry, a truth that is explained by one writer as due to the presence of the tool marks of the craftsman in the case of cut stone structures and its absence in concrete. The tool marks express to the observer the human labor required to create the object, and give it a human interest.

The greatest architectural defect of concrete, however, is doubtless the lack of color effect in its finished surfaces, and especially the lack of color variety. The uniformity of color and texture of concrete surfaces is monotonous and displeasing.

This loss of the charm of the natural stone wall, however, is balanced by the economy of the material, allowing its use in many places, especially for small bridges, where natural stone could not be used or afforded and where cheap, unsightly steel trusses would formerly have been built.

In all fairness it should be stated, however, that the ugliness of the small steel bridge is due, not to any inherent defect of the material, but to the utter lack of any attention to considerations of beauty on the part of designers, such lack being caused by the former commercialization of the art, practically all designs for small structures, and many for large ones, being made by the fabricating companies, under competitive conditions that precluded any consideration of art or taste. Such a system, while possibly resulting in the greatest economy of first cost, is essentially bad, because it results not only in the total elimination of artistic considerations, but also results in the production of structures that are weak and short-lived, and more expensive in the long run than would be the case if better designs were adopted at perhaps somewhat greater first cost.

Furthermore, a beautiful and pleasingly designed bridge has a certain value to a community not easily expressed in dollars, but which pays dividends in pride in one's community, a pride which contributes to human happiness and contentment.

Quoting the editor of "The Builder" (Aug. 27, 1926), "The Engineer's artistic failures occur when he has not interested himself in the appearance of his building and allows himself to be governed blindly by economy."

In studying these illustrations of concrete bridges, it will be seen that, in order to obtain the most pleasing results, concrete must be treated as a different material than natural stone and that the obvious forms of cut stone masonry should not be imitated in using the plastic material. The earlier examples committed this error extensively, but later designs are better.

, , ,

One of the first large concrete bridges to be built in this country is The Connecticut Avenue Bridge at Washington, D. C., completed in 1904, after designs by George S. Morison, noted American bridge engineer and designer of many railroad bridges; and built under the direction of W. J. Douglas, engineer, and

E. P. Casey, architect. This bridge is 1341 feet long, 120 feet high and 52 feet wide. It contains seven semi-circular arches, five of which have a span of 150 feet. These arches carry six small spandrel arches, also semi-circular. The parapet is composed of concrete posts with a bronze railing. The material of which the concrete of this imposing work is made is crushed granite, and exposed surfaces were carefully tooled when cured, exposing the aggregates of the concrete. The quoins of the piers were made of precast blocks of concrete.

Considered either from the viewpoint of the engineer or the architect, this work must be conceded to be one of the finest, if not the best executed concrete bridge yet built. After twenty-two years of service, it exhibits no defects or deterioration. (Plates CXXXII & CXXXIII.)

, , ,

The Walnut Lane Bridge in Fairmount Park, Philadelphia, completed in 1908 after designs by H. H. Quimby, has a main span of 233 feet, a height of 147 feet and width of 60 feet. Its setting, being located over a parkway, adds greatly to its beauty. (Plate CXXXIV.)

, , ,

The Bridge over Rocky River, near Cleveland, Ohio, completed in 1910 after designs by A. M. Felgate, is quite similar in conception to the Walnut Lane Bridge, but more massive in design and of longer span. At the time of its construction, this bridge held the record for length of span for a masonry arch bridge, a record since broken by several structures. The main arch span is 280 feet opening and comprises two massive ribs, not reinforced.

The length over all is 708 feet and the width 60 feet. The massiveness of these arch rings is in harmony with the span and heavy superstructure, a feature lacking in so many reinforced concrete arch bridges, the designers of which seem to attempt the greatest possible attenuity of the arch rib. In the construction of this bridge, a facing mixture composed of specially selected aggregate (crushed granite) was used for all exposed surfaces. (Plate CXXXV.)

The Cherry Street Bridge over the Maumee River, at Toledo, Ohio, completed in 1912 after plans originally drawn by The Osborn Engineering Co., of Cleveland, and later modified and executed by Ralph Modjeski, has a length of 1217 feet and width of 80 feet and comprises ten arches, elliptical in shape, and having maximum spans of 108 feet at the center, diminishing in length toward the ends. At the center is a bascule span providing 200 feet clear opening for the passage of boats, and carried on two massive abutment piers. These center piers have octagonal ends, which were intended to carry ornamental towers designed by the late Arnold W. Brunner, but not built owing to lack of funds, an omission which ruins the appearance of so many of our monumental structures. The excuse is always made that these ornamental features are not strictly necessary, which, of course, has to be admitted if it be admitted that beauty of form is not a necessity to civilized man. The Cherry Street Bridge is described in the Transactions of the American Society of Civil Engineers, 1915. (Plates CXXXVI & CXXXVII.)

The King Avenue Bridge over the Olentangy River, at Columbus, Ohio, built in 1912 and 1913 from designs by W. J. Watson and Walter Braun, comprises four elliptical arch spans of the solid spandrel type. The arches

CHERRY STREET BRIDGE, TOLEDO, O.
COLUMN DESIGN BY ARNOLD W. BRUNNER

have a clear opening of 85 feet each. The length over all is 429 feet 9 inches and the width 47 feet. This bridge may be considered as typical of its kind, although greater pains have been taken to obtain pleasing lines than is usual in this class of structure. The essential features may be described as the use of perfect ellipses for the intradosal curves, curved cutwaters for the piers, curved retaining walls at the abutments and a carefully executed parapet. Another feature of this bridge is the light color, almost white, obtained by the use of selected aggregates (white limestone) for the concrete. No attempt to imitate cut stone masonry is made.

Some details of the King Avenue Bridge at Columbus, Ohio, illustrate methods of treating cutwaters and piers. The slight projection of the pilasters, only a few inches, is just enough to provide a line for the necessary expansion joints. The treatment of the wing walls at the abutments, which are curved instead of straight, is a detail not expensive to carry out in concrete. (Plate CXXXIX.)

ɤ ɤ ɤ

A concrete Viaduct at Willoughby, Ohio, carries the Buffalo-Cleveland Road, a heavily traveled highway, over the valley of the Chagrin River, on a bridge 1080 feet long, containing nine arch spans of 100 feet each and two 50 feet each. The parapets and lamp

KING AVENUE BRIDGE, COLUMBUS, O.—DETAIL

standards are of cast concrete, using red granite aggregates, the surface being scrubbed while the concrete was green in order to expose the granite. This bridge was completed in 1921, after designs by W. J. Watson and W. P. Brown, with M. P. Potter as collaborating architect. (Plates CXLII & CXLIII.)

ɤ ɤ ɤ

A concrete bridge of the New York Central Railroad at Willoughby is a good example

KING AVENUE BRIDGE, COLUMBUS, O.—DETAIL

THIRD AVENUE BRIDGE, COLUMBUS, O,—DETAIL

of the massive type of concrete arch of the ribbed type, as adapted to heavy railroad work. This bridge was designed by Samuel Rockwell, chief engineer, and O. W. Irwin, assistant. (Plate CXLIV.)

, , ,

Richmond, Virginia, has a historic bridge over the James River known as the Mayo's Bridge, a bridge bearing this name having existed at this site from early colonial times. In 1911, it was decided to replace the old structure, which was too light for the increasingly heavy traffic, with a new and modern concrete structure, and a board of three engineers, consisting of the late Col. C. P. E. Burgwyn, Chas. E. Bolling and W. J. Watson, was appointed to report upon plans. Competitive plans were received and the design submitted by The Concrete Steel Engineering Company of New York was selected. This bridge is 1775 feet long over all, and contains eighteen arches, having a clear span of 71 feet and a rise of only 7 feet. The project was completed in 1914. In no way does the

design of this structure involve concrete in imitation of cut stone masonry forms. (Plates CXLV & CXLVI.)

, , ,

At Akron, Ohio, there stands a reinforced concrete highway bridge over the Cuyahoga River Gorge, which is one of the highest structures of this kind in the world, its deck being 192 feet above the water. On account of its great height and park-like setting, in a deep wooded ravine, this bridge presents a striking profile. Its length is 781 feet 9 inches over all and it comprises five semi-circular arches, each 127 feet in length from center to center of high, hollow piers. The engineer was W. J. Watson. This bridge was built in 1915. (Plate CXLVII.)

, , ,

The concrete viaduct carrying the Cumberland Valley R. R. over the Susquehanna River at Harrisburg, Pa., was built in 1915-16, from designs by the Railroad Company's engineers. This massive bridge is 4000 feet long and comprises 45 spans of about 76 feet each.

RAILING AND POST OF WILLOUGHBY BRIDGE

The work was carried out in two longitudinal halves, traffic on the railroad not being interrupted by the construction. (Plate CXLVIII.)

ꞌ ꞌ ꞌ

On the Florida East Coast Railway, between Miami and Key West, a very long concrete bridge connecting two keys, famous as the Long Key Viaduct, was completed in 1907. The design is not unusual and is devoid of architectural treatment, but its great length of two miles and the boldness of the undertaking, the site being in the open sea, are noteworthy, and have caused it to be classed as a wonderful engineering accomplishment.

ꞌ ꞌ ꞌ

At Dayton, Ohio, a number of imposing bridges of reinforced concrete cross the Miami and Mad Rivers, some of which were built before the great flood of 1913, that destroyed a large part of the city, and were but little damaged thereby.

A recent structure by Chamberlain & Smith, architects, of Dayton, is unique in design. (Plate CXLIX.)

ꞌ ꞌ ꞌ

The longest concrete bridge yet built in a single span was recently completed over the River Seine, below Paris, boasting the unprecedented span of 450 feet. It possesses little architectural merit, and it is somewhat puzzling to one that the French engineers and architects, who have built the most beautiful stone bridges in the world, seem to make so little effort to obtain equally pleasing designs in concrete. (Plate CL.)

ꞌ ꞌ ꞌ

The Tunkhannock Viaduct, on the D., L. & W. R. R., is the most stupendous achievement in concrete bridge construction yet attempted.

This great structure is 2375 feet in length, and 240 feet in height above the ground, while its foundations extend another 60 feet below the ground surface, a total height of 300 feet, easily the world's record for this kind of a bridge. The design is by George J. Ray, chief engineer, D., L. & W. R. R., and the work was carried out by Flickwir & Bush, contractors, and completed in 1916. About 162,000 cubic yards of concrete were used in its construction. (Plate CLI.)

The division of the arch ring into imitation voussoirs is especially to be criticised in this case, as the proportions of the arch rings make them obviously false. Would not the piers look better if the jointing also had been omitted, or so designed as not to simulate cut stone forms?

Another detail used in the design of the Tunkhannock Viaduct and in many other recent bridges, which is evidently superfluous and therefore questionable, is the use of the projecting cap at the top of the spandrel posts. In most cases, the design would actually be much improved by the omission of this expensive detail. This statement is well illustrated by a comparison of this detail of the Tunkhannock Bridge with that used on the Connecticut Avenue Bridge at Washington.

The D., L. & W. R. R. has built many very beautiful concrete bridges in recent years, that over the Delaware River just below the Delaware Water Gap being perhaps the most striking. This bridge has a length of 1450 feet and is composed of a series of 150-foot spans of the open spandrel type. It was completed in 1910. Lincoln Bush and George J. Ray were the engineers in charge. (Plate CLII.)

The Washington Street Memorial Bridge at Wilmington, Delaware, is a fine example of the modern concrete highway bridge, one of the best yet executed. The design is by B. H. Davis, engineer, in collaboration with V. W. Torbert, architect. This bridge comprises a single arch span, of the ribbed, open spandrel type, flanked on each side by two arches of the solid spandrel type. At each end of the main span are massive pylons supporting memorial tablets, and smaller pylons are placed at the ends of the bridge. (Plates CLIII, CLIV & CLV.)

✔ ✔ ✔

It has been suggested that the arch ring and the piers also of a concrete bridge should be divided to indicate just how the sections were placed.

The charm of stone masonry is largely due to the fact that the jointing expresses the manner in which the work is done. False joints in stone masonry, therefore, are generally avoided. Should not this principle be applied to concrete masonry?

Stone masonry is laid up of separate blocks, while concrete is a plastic material and should not imitate the structural forms and details of stone block masonry which are required by the nature of the material, but are not required by concrete. Authorities on architectural history tell us that the dentils used in classical structures are probably imitations, in stone, of the ends of timber rafters used in still more ancient structures. Dentils, however, when used as corbels, serve a useful purpose in supporting an overhanging cornice or coping, and they have been extensively so used in bridges in the past, and quite effectively. When the dentil is introduced into concrete masonry, however, it does not seem to express this function as well as it did in stone masonry. In concrete designs it is seldom used as a structural member, its function becoming evidently purely decorative.

Concrete is essentially monolithic, and designs executed in concrete should, properly it would seem, express this fact, not conceal it, and this expression can be conveyed by the use of plastic forms, mouldings and curved surfaces. In spite of much that has been quoted herein about unnecessary decoration as applied to bridges, a certain amount of plastic decorative design helps to express to the observer the nature of the material.

Proper treatment of the surface is also needed to express the nature of concrete. In stone masonry this is accomplished by the tooling necessary to prepare the blocks for use. In the case of concrete, which is composed of cement and small pieces of stone, if it is desired to show these elements, surface treatment is required, which is not a constructive necessity, but purely a finishing operation.

✔ ✔ ✔

The Dumbarton Bridge, on Q Street, Washington, D. C., a very unique structure, carries Q Street over Rock Creek Park on a curve. The spandrels are tooled to give a coarse texture to the concrete. The arches are semicircular in shape, being outlined with a narrow ring of smooth finished concrete. The end posts are surmounted by heavy cast bronze buffaloes designed by A. Phimister Proctor, sculptor. The architect was Glenn Brown. (Plate CLVI.)

✔ ✔ ✔

The new bridge over the Monongahela River

at Fairmont, West Virginia, claims especial merit in the treatment of the railing, the combined trolley and lighting poles and the overhanging recesses. The design is by The Concrete-Steel Engineering Company of New York, William Meuser, engineer. (Plate CLVII.)

⁊ ⁊ ⁊

A bridge at San Diego, California, called the Cabrillo Bridge, consists of a series of severely plain concrete arches and formed one of the principal approaches to the Panama-California Exposition held in 1915. This bridge was greatly admired by visitors to the Exposition. It is utterly devoid of any attempt at ornamentation and practically without detail, yet beautiful in its simplicity. It is composed of seven semicircular arch spans of 56 feet opening each, and has a total length of 946 feet. The designer is Frank P. Allen, Jr., in collaboration with Cram, Goodhue & Ferguson, architects. (Plate CLVIII.)

⁊ ⁊ ⁊

The Cappelen Bridge over the Mississippi River at Minneapolis, Minn., contains the longest reinforced concrete arch yet constructed in America, 400 feet in length. This bridge is named for the late F. W. Cappelen, City Engineer of Minneapolis, and is 1100 feet long, comprising one span of 400 feet, two of 199 feet, and two of 55 feet opening, carrying a 40-foot roadway and two 8-foot walks. (Plate CLIX.)

At St. Paul, Minnesota, Messrs. Toltz, King and Day, architects and engineers of that city, have built a reinforced concrete bridge over the Mississippi River, known as the Robert Street Bridge, which comprises a clear span of 244 feet in its total length of 1900 feet and presents some unusual architectural details. (Plate CLX.)

Pont Butin at Geneva, Switzerland

A bridge has recently been completed at Geneva, Switzerland, which illustrates the modern tendency among European engineers and architects toward the use of concrete and stone masonry in combination, the former as a strictly structural material, and the latter for facing purposes. This bridge is known as the Pont Butin, and spans the River Rhône. Its length over all is 276 meters, comprising five semicircular arches with clear spans of 48 meters. These five arches carry the railway tracks and a series of twenty-five smaller arches which form the upper deck, used for a highway 15 meters wide. The height is 52 meters. The entire structure is of reinforced concrete with a facing of limestone and granite. The engineers in charge were M. M. Bollinger and Company of Zurich, and the architect collaborating was M. Garcin, of Geneva. (Plate CLXII.)

Other modern European masonry bridges, constructed partly or wholly of concrete, and worthy of study, are the Pont de Malling, a railway bridge in Lorraine, and two bridges at Rome, known as the Ponte Cavour and the Ponte Umberto. (Plates CLXIII, CLXIV & CLXV.)

⁊ ⁊ ⁊

A bridge of unique design was built by the Westchester County Park Commission in 1915, at Scarsdale, New York, from plans by Delano and Aldrich, architects, in collaboration with the engineers of the Commission, of which J. Downer is chief engineer.

This bridge is on a curve and the spans are supported on circular piers placed on the center line of the roadway. (Plate CLXVI.)

So few American bridges have the charm of old historical interest or of ancient folklore that attaches to many bridges in Europe, that advantage should be taken of every opportunity to lend interest to the more important structures by naming them in commemoration of historic events that took place in the locality, or by the name of the community which they serve, or occasionally, the name of a noted architect or engineer.

The Key Bridge at Washington, recently completed, crosses the Potomac River near the site of the home of Francis Scott Key, the composer of "The Star Spangled Banner"; the proposed Arlington Bridge will form the principal approach from the City to Arlington National Cemetery; the Cappelen Bridge at Minneapolis (already described) was so named in honor of a city engineer who served the municipality faithfully for many years and well merited the recognition. The California State Highway Commission has named one of its most beautiful structures after the late Harlan D. Miller, for many years its bridge engineer. How much such a plan adds to the human interest of a bridge. (Plates CLXVII, CLXVIII, CLXIX & CLXX.)

The ordinary railroad bridge is seldom interesting from any standpoint except that of strict utility, safety and economy, yet quite often this type of structure may be greatly improved, architecturally, without increase of cost. This was the case with the two crossings of streets by the tracks of the Cleveland & Youngstown R. R., and the New York Central R. R. in Cleveland, shown by plates. The tracks are carried over the streets by massive concrete arches, designed for the heaviest modern loading, with no attempt whatever at ornamentation, such interest as they have being due entirely to their mass and proportion. These structures cost no more than much less attractive bridges of steel would have cost, although very pleasing results can be obtained, if desired, with the latter material. Unfortunately, in so many cases, the desire to make such structures good-looking does not exist, either in the minds of the owners or of the designers, or, if it does exist, is immediately dismissed with the idea that anything that is good-looking is necessarily more expensive and extravagant or wasteful. (Plates CLXXI, CLXXII, CLXXIII & CLXXIV.)

⸙ ⸙ ⸙

Good architecture in bridges is not and should not be confined to the larger projects, but is of equal importance to the small structure. As examples of what may be

RAILING DESIGN BY C. A. P. TURNER

accomplished in the design and construction of small highway bridges in concrete, note the illustrations of such structures at Niagara Falls, Ontario; Lynchburg, Virginia; Montclair, New Jersey; at Piedmont and at Riverside, California; at Cincinnati, Ohio; at Jacksonville, Florida; Gaston County, North Carolina, etc. All of these are small, inexpensive structures. (Plates CLXXV, CLXXVI, CLXXVII, CLXXVIII, CLXXIX, CLXXX, CLXXXI, CLXXXII, CLXXXIII, CLXXXIV, CLXXXV, CLXXXVI, CLXXXVII, CLXXXVIII.)

Some Proposed Bridges

Studies are now being made looking to the construction of the most stupendous bridge ever built—that over the Hudson River at Fort Lee, New Jersey. A tentative report has already been made by a commission of the Port of New York Authority, composed of O. H. Ammann, W. W. Drinker, Prof. W. H. Burr, engineers, and Cass Gilbert, architect. This tentative report contemplates the construction of a suspension bridge comprising a central span of 3500 feet, twice that of the Philadelphia-Camden Bridge, the longest yet built. The towers would be 650 feet high, nearly 100 feet higher than the Washington Monument at Washington. The preliminary drawings by Cass Gilbert show masonry towers (encasing the steel skeleton) and a conception of surpassing beauty, although the use of encasing masonry that no longer serves a useful purpose may be open to criticism.

The proposed bridge over Kill von Kull, to be built by the Port of New York Authority, will contain a steel arch span of 1650 feet span, equaling that at Sydney Harbor, Australia. Prof. W. H. Burr and Gen. George W. Goethals are consulting engineers for the Kill von Kull Bridge, and Cass Gilbert is architect.

Modern Opening Bridges

One of the difficult problems confronting the modern bridge engineer is that of obtaining a pleasing treatment of the opening bridge, a type generally considered to be inherently and hopelessly ugly, and which many engineers spend no effort to make anything else. Recent drawbridges built and now being built in Chicago, however, possess distinct architectural merit. Among those now completed are the Michigan Avenue Bridge, the

WEST SUMMIT STREET BRIDGE, WARREN, O.—DETAIL

ROBERT STREET BRIDGE, ST. PAUL, MINN.

Probably the most ornate opening bridge ever built is the Tower Bridge over the Thames at London, opened for traffic in June, 1894. This is the joint work of J. W. Barry, as engineer, and Horace Jones, as architect. The length of the bridge is about 800 feet, composed of a channel span of 200 feet clear opening, and two fixed flanking spans of the suspension type. The very elaborate towers have a skeleton of steel, encased in granite, stone and brick. An unusual feature is the provision of a foot walk at a clearance of 141 feet over the river, for use when the draw is open, and reached by elevators in the towers.

The Anacostia Bridge at Washington has a very neatly designed bascule span of 100

West Madison Street Bridge and the Franklyn Street Bridge.

These bridges are designed in collaboration between the engineers of the Department of Bridges of the City and the architect of the City Plan Commission and the results speak for themselves.

The treatment of the approaches to the Michigan Avenue Bridge is very elaborate, as befits such an important crossing, and includes provision for statuary on the four main pylons and for wide plazas.

E. H. Bennett is consulting architect to the Plan Commission and to him is much of the credit due for the results obtained.

At Wilhelmshaven, Germany, there has recently been constructed a double swing bridge of unique design, the trusses combining the cantilever and suspension principles.

GLENS FALLS, N. Y. BRIDGE STAIRS

feet clear channel opening. This bridge, consisting of a series of steel arch spans, was built in 1902, under the direction of Col. John Biddle, U. S. A., and W. J. Douglas, engineer of bridges.

The Cherry Street Bridge over the Maumee River at Toledo, Ohio, comprises a bascule channel span with a clear opening of 200 feet flanked on each side by heavy concrete piers which conceal the operating parts, as is the case at the Anacostia Bridge. The effect of the Toledo Bridge is marred by the omission of the pylons planned by the late Arnold Brunner. (Plates CXCI, CXCII, CXCIII, CXCIV, CXCV, CXCVI, CXCVII, CXCVIII & CXCIX.)

PLATE CXXXII—WASHINGTON, D. C.—CONNECTICUT AVENUE BRIDGE—GEO. S. MORISON & W. J. DOUGLAS, ENGINEERS—1904

PLATE CXXXIII—WASHINGTON, D. C.—CONNECTICUT AVENUE BRIDGE—COMPLETED 1904
GEO. S. MORISON & W. J. DOUGLAS, ENGINEERS

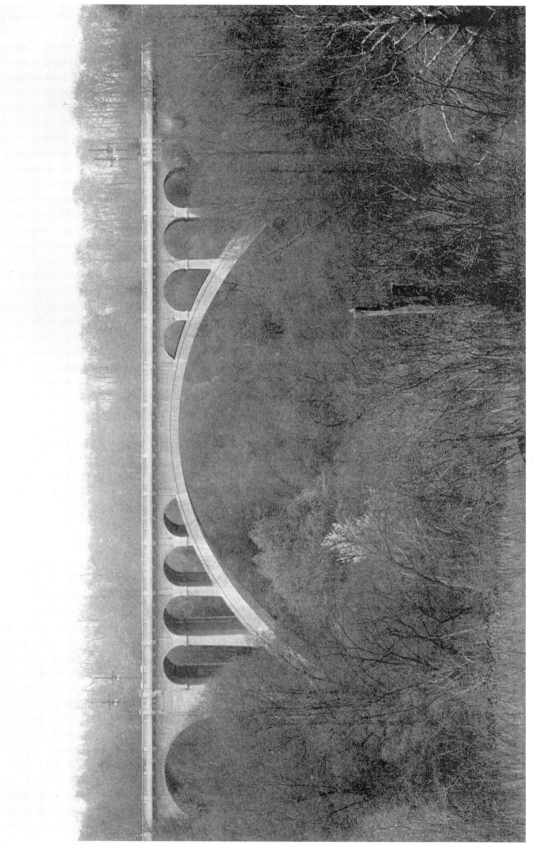

PLATE CXXXIV—PHILADELPHIA, PA.—WALNUT LANE BRIDGE—H. H. QUIMBY, ENGINEER—1908

PLATE CXXXV—CLEVELAND, OHIO—CONCRETE ARCH OF 280-FOOT SPAN OVER ROCKY RIVER
A. M. FELGATE, DESIGNING ENGINEER. W. J. WATSON, CONSULTING ENGINEER

PLATE CXXXVI—TOLEDO, OHIO—CHERRY STREET BRIDGE OVER THE MAUMEE RIVER—1912—THE OSBORN ENGINEERING CO., DESIGNING ENGINEERS. RALPH MODJESKI, CONSULTING ENGINEER

PLATE CXXXVII—TOLEDO, OHIO—CHERRY STREET BRIDGE OVER THE MAUMEE RIVER—DECK VIEW—1912
THE OSBORN ENGINEERING CO., DESIGNERS. RALPH MODJESKI, CONSULTING ENGINEER

PLATE CXXXVIII—ALLENTOWN, PA.—CONCRETE HIGHWAY BRIDGE DESIGNED BY B. H. DAVIS

PLATE CXXXIX—COLUMBUS, OHIO—KING AVENUE BRIDGE OVER THE OLENTANGY RIVER—1914
WALTER BRAUN & WILBUR J. WATSON, ENGINEERS

PLATE CXL—COLUMBUS, OHIO—THIRD STREET BRIDGE OVER OLENTANGY RIVER—1919—WILBUR J. WATSON, ENGINEER

PLATE CXLI—COLUMBUS, OHIO—BROAD STREET BRIDGE OVER THE SCIOTO RIVER—1921
BRAUN, KNOLLMAN & FLEMING, ENGINEERS

PLATE CXLII—WILLOUGHBY, OHIO—HIGHWAY BRIDGE OVER THE CHAGRIN RIVER—1921—WILBUR J. WATSON AND
W. P. BROWN, ENGINEERS. M. P. POTTER, CONSULTING ARCHITECT

PLATE CXLIII—WILLOUGHBY, OHIO—BRIDGE OVER THE CHAGRIN RIVER—1921—DECK VIEW—WILBUR J. WATSON
AND W. P. BROWN, ENGINEERS. M. P. POTTER, CONSULTING ARCHITECT

PLATE CXLIV—WILLOUGHBY, OHIO—RAILWAY BRIDGE OVER THE CHAGRIN RIVER—SAMUEL ROCKWELL AND
O. W. IRWIN, ENGINEERS

PLATE CXLV—RICHMOND, VA.—MAYO'S BRIDGE OVER THE JAMES RIVER—1913—DESIGN BY THE CONCRETE-STEEL ENGINEERING CO.—C. P. E. BURGWYN, CHAS. BOLLING AND WILBUR WATSON, CONSULTING ENGINEERS

PLATE CXLVI—RICHMOND, VA.—MAYO'S BRIDGE OVER THE JAMES RIVER—1913—DESIGNED BY THE CONCRETE-STEEL ENGINEERING CO.—C. P. E. BURGWYN, CHAS. BOLLING AND WILBUR WATSON, CONSULTING ENGINEERS.

PLATE CXLVII—AKRON, OHIO—BRIDGE OVER CUYAHOGA RIVER—192 FEET HIGH—1915—WILBUR J. WATSON, ENGINEER

PLATE CXLVIII.—HARRISBURG PA.—RAILROAD BRIDGE OVER THE SUSQUEHANNA RIVER—1916—4000 FEET LONG

PLATE CXLIX—DAYTON, OHIO—ISLAND PARK BRIDGE—E. R. SMITH & J. J. CHAMBERLAIN, ARCHITECTS & ENGINEERS—1926

PHOTO BY HOWARD WELLER, DAYTON

PLATE CL—FRANCE—BRIDGE OVER THE SEINE—430-FOOT SPAN—E. FREYSSINET, ENGINEER—1924

PHOTOGRAPH BY UNDERWOOD & UNDERWOOD, NEW YORK

PLATE CLI—TUNKHANNOCK VIADUCT—D. L. & W. R. R.—GEO. J. RAY, CHIEF ENGINEER—1916

PLATE CLII—DELAWARE WATER GAP—CONCRETE VIADUCT OF D., L. & W. R. R. OVER THE DELAWARE RIVER—BUILT 1910
LINCOLN BUSH & G. J. RAY, ENGINEERS

PLATE CLIII—WILMINGTON, DEL.—WASHINGTON STREET MEMORIAL BRIDGE—B. H. DAVIS, ENGINEER
V. W. TORBERT, CONSULTING ARCHITECT

PLATE CLIV—WILMINGTON, DEL.—WASHINGTON STREET MEMORIAL BRIDGE—1922—B. H. DAVIS, ENGINEER
V. W. TORBERT, ARCHITECT

PLATE CLV—WILMINGTON, DEL.—WASHINGTON STREET MEMORIAL BRIDGE
B. H. DAVIS, ENGINEER; V. W. TORBERT, ARCHITECT

PLATE CLVI—WASHINGTON, D. C.—"Q" STREET BRIDGE—GLENN BROWN, ARCHITECT.   A. PHIMISTER PROCTOR, SCULPTOR

PLATE CLVII.—FAIRMONT, W. VA.—CONCRETE BRIDGE OVER THE MONONGAHELA RIVER—1918—THE CONCRETE-STEEL
ENGINEERING CO., NEW YORK, ENGINEERS

PLATE CLVIII—SAN DIEGO, CAL.—CABRILLO BRIDGE—1915—FRANK P. ALLEN, JR., ENGINEER
CRAM, GOODHUE & FERGUSON, ARCHITECTS

PLATE CLIX—MINNEAPOLIS, MINN.—THE CAPPELEN BRIDGE OVER THE MISSISSIPPI RIVER—400-FOOT SPAN
F. W. CAPPELEN, CITY ENGINEER

PLATE CLX—ST. PAUL, MINN.—ROBERT STREET BRIDGE OVER THE MISSISSIPPI RIVER—1926
TOLTZ, KING & DAY, INC., ENGINEERS AND ARCHITECTS

PLATE CLXI—HAVERHILL, MASS.—CONCRETE BRIDGE OVER THE MERRIMAC RIVER—GEO. F. SWAIN, ENGINEER

PLATE CLXII—GENEVA—PONT BUTIN, SÛR LE RHONE—COMPLETED 1926—M. GARCIN, ARCHITECT

M. M. BOLLINGER & CO., ENGINEERS

PHOTO BY JULLIEN FRERES, GENEVA

PLATE CLXIII—LORRAINE—PONT DE MALLING SUR LA MOSELLE—M. PAUL SÉJOURNÉ, ENGINEER

PLATE CLXIV—ROME—PONTE CAVOUR—1902

PHOTO BY BROGI, FLORENCE

PLATE CLXV—ROME—PONTE UMBERTO—1899
PHOTO FROM ED. BROGI

PLATE CLXVI—SCARSDALE, N. Y.—WESTCHESTER COUNTY PARK BRIDGE—1915—JAY DOWNER, CHIEF ENGINEER
DELANO & ALDRICH, CONSULTING ARCHITECTS.   ARTHUR G. HAYDEN, DESIGNING ENGINEER

PLATE CLXVII—WASHINGTON, D. C.—THE FRANCIS SCOTT KEY BRIDGE OVER THE POTOMAC RIVER—1925

PLATE CLXVIII

PLATE CLXIX
CALIFORNIA STATE HIGHWAY BRIDGES—MODERN CONCRETE
HARLAN D. MILLER, STATE BRIDGE ENGINEER

PLATE CLXX—CALIFORNIA—HIGHWAY BRIDGE—DESIGNED BY HARLAN D. MILLER, STATE BRIDGE ENGINEER

PLATE CLXXI—CLEVELAND, OHIO—CONCRETE ARCHES CARRYING FOUR TRACK RAILROAD OVER STREETS—1916
WILBUR J. WATSON, ENGINEER

PLATE CLXXII—CLEVELAND, OHIO—RAILWAY BRIDGE OVER STREET—1916—DESIGNED BY W. J. WATSON, ENGINEER

PLATE CLXXIII—RICHMOND, VA.—RAILROAD BRIDGE OVER THE JAMES RIVER—J. E. GREINER & CO., ENGINEERS

PLATE CLXXIV—HERKIMER, N.Y.—BRIDGE OVER WEST CANADA CREEK—1902—THE OSBORN ENGINEERING CO., ENGINEERS

PHOTO BY DETROIT PUBLISHING CO.

PLATE CLXXV—NIAGARA FALLS, ONT.—RAILWAY BRIDGE IN QUEEN VICTORIA PARK—1905
PHOTO BY W. J. W.

PLATE CLXXVI—CINCINNATI, OHIO—BRIDGE DESIGNED BY GARBER & WOODWARD, ARCHITECTS

PLATE CLXXVII—LYNCHBURG, VA.—BRIDGE CARRYING FIFTH STREET OVER SOUTHERN RY.—1909
H. L. SHANER, CITY ENGINEER. WILBUR J. WATSON, CONSULTING ENGINEER

PLATE CLXXVIII—LYNCHBURG, VA.—D STREET VIADUCT—DETAIL—JAS. H. FUERTES, ENGINEER—1915

PLATE CLXXIX—JACKSONVILLE, FLA.—CONCRETE PILE BRIDGE OVER LITTLE POTSBURG CREEK—1910

DESIGN AND PHOTO BY WILBUR J. WATSON

PLATE CLXXX—A SMALL CONCRETE HIGHWAY BRIDGE IN NORTH CAROLINA—DESIGNED BY WILBUR J. WATSON

PLATE CLXXXI—WARREN, OHIO—CONCRETE BRIDGE OVER THE MAHONING RIVER ON SUMMIT STREET—1916
WILBUR J. WATSON, ENGINEER

PLATE CLXXXII—CHESTER, PA.—MEMORIAL BRIDGE—1926—CLARENCE W. BRAZER, ARCHITECT

PLATE CLXXXIII-A—MONTCLAIR, N. J.—CONCRETE PARK BRIDGE—PARAPETS OF PRECAST CONCRETE

PHOTO FROM ONONDAGA LITHOLITE CO., SYRACUSE, N. Y.

PLATE CLXXXIII-B—MONTCLAIR, N. J.—CONCRETE PARK BRIDGE

PHOTO FROM ONONDAGA LITHOLITE CO., SYRACUSE, N. Y.

PLATE CLXXXIV-A—PIEDMONT, CALIF.—SMALL CONCRETE HIGHWAY BRIDGE—1914

PLATE CLXXXIV-B—PIEDMONT, CALIF.—SMALL CONCRETE ARCH BRIDGE—1914

PLATE CLXXXV—RIVERSIDE, CALIFORNIA—BRIDGE PORTALS IN MISSION STYLE

PHOTO BY UNDERWOOD & UNDERWOOD, NEW YORK

PLATE CLXXXVI—CINCINNATI, OHIO—FOOT BRIDGE AT EAST SIDE HIGH SCHOOL
GARBER & WOODWARD, ARCHITECTS

PLATE CLXXXVII—DAYTON, OHIO—FINDLAY STREET BRIDGE OVER THE MAD RIVER—BUILT 1926
WALTER BRAUN & WILBUR J. WATSON, ENGINEERS

PLATE CLXXXVIII—CLEVELAND, OHIO—HILLIARD BRIDGE OVER ROCKY RIVER—A. M. FELGATE, ENGINEER—1926

PLATE CLXXXIX—BAVARIA—DETAIL OF CONCRETE RAILWAY BRIDGE—M. BEUTEL, ENGINEER-

PLATE CXC—BOSTON, MASS.—CONCRETE BRIDGE OVER CHARLES RIVER—DETAIL

PLATE CXCI—ST. AUGUSTINE, FLA.—J. E. GREINER & CO., ENGINEERS—1927

PLATE CXCII—WILHELMSHAVEN, GERMANY—DOUBLE SWING BRIDGE

PLATE CXCIII—LONDON—THE TOWER BRIDGE—J. W. BARRY, ENGINEER. HORACE JONES, ARCHITECT—1894

PLATE CXCIV—WASHINGTON, D. C.—ANACOSTIA BRIDGE—1902—COL. JOHN BIDDLE, U. S. A., & W. J. DOUGLAS, ENGINEERS

PLATE CXCV—TOLEDO, OHIO—CHERRY STREET BRIDGE OVER THE MAUMEE RIVER—1912—THE OSBORN ENGINEERING CO., DESIGNING ENGINEERS. RALPH MODJESKI, CONSULTING ENGINEER

PLATE CXCVI—WASHINGTON, D. C.—THE ARLINGTON MEMORIAL BRIDGE OVER THE POTOMAC—BASCULE SPAN
COL. C. O. SHERRILL, CHIEF ENGINEER; JOHN L. NAGLE, DESIGNING ENGINEER; W. J. DOUGLAS, CONSULTING ENGINEER.
McKIM, MEAD & WHITE, ARCHITECTS
UNDER CONSTRUCTION (1927)

PLATE CXCVII—CHICAGO, ILL.—DRAWBRIDGE OVER THE CHICAGO RIVER ON MICHIGAN AVE.—DESIGNED BY THE
DEPARTMENT OF BRIDGES, CHICAGO. E. H. BENNETT, CONSULTING ARCHITECT

PLATE CXCVIII—CHICAGO, ILL.—WEST MADISON STREET BRIDGE OVER THE CHICAGO RIVER. DESIGNED BY THE
DEPARTMENT OF BRIDGES OF THE CITY OF CHICAGO. E. H. BENNETT, CONSULTING ARCHITECT

PLATE CXCIX—CHICAGO, ILL.—FRANKLIN STREET BRIDGE OVER THE CHICAGO RIVER. DESIGNED BY THE DEPARTMENT OF BRIDGES OF THE CITY OF CHICAGO. E. H. BENNETT, CONSULTING ARCHITECT

POSTWORD

WHAT will be the Bridge Architecture of the future? We have reviewed briefly the past history of the art and its present condition, and have seen that the principal factors controlling the development have been—

First: The general state of development of the people.

Second: The standards of technical and artistic skill.

Third: The materials available.

Fourth: The methods of transportation.

Applying these factors to the immediate future, we may safely assume that the general material development of civilized peoples will not recede, and there are unmistakable evidences of a greater appreciation of things artistic and pleasing to the eye. The new demand will lead to higher standards of artistic taste, and especially as applied to the implements of production, trade and transportation, which in the past have required only technical skill.

The materials available for bridges, which in the past included successively timber, then stone masonry, then iron and steel and lastly the combination of concrete and steel, are now all available at one time and may all be employed in a single structure. To those engineers who have made a most careful study of all materials, it seems certain that stone masonry will continue to be the material par-excellence for the best and most monumental structures, when its properties will allow its use. It seems extremely doubtful that reinforced concrete will displace exposed structural steel for many bridges, especially those of long span. Doubtless, our scientists will soon produce for us a non-corrodible steel or steel alloy, which will reduce the present high maintenance cost of steel bridges and will probably tend toward a return to the light, airy forms which this material permits and which has a charm all its own.

The newest material, reinforced concrete, has, as shown by the illustrations, been in use only about a quarter of a century, in which time it has largely displaced stone masonry and steel for bridges of moderate span and for long viaducts. This material possesses great possibilities for artistic treatment, but so far most of the work executed therein has followed and imitated the exterior forms of stone masonry or exposed steel instead of frankly expressing its own peculiar and useful nature.

There is a tendency among engineers today toward extreme specialization, certain engineers specializing in reinforced concrete work, some in steel and others in other materials. While there may be some advantages in such specialization on the part of *assistant* designers, it stands to reason that the bridge engineer or architect, on whose judgment rests the decision as to the proper materials to use for a certain structure, must be a man thoroughly familiar with all materials and prejudiced in regard to none. Above the specialist must stand the architect-engineer of broad mind and broad training if good designs are to be obtained.

Methods of transportation change from time to time, requiring great changes in the design of bridges. We see the narrow structures of the Romans, designed for chariots and cavalry and infantry, the still narrower roadways of the Middle Ages, some of them too narrow for vehicles of any kind. Then, we see the revolution in bridge construction brought about by the invention of the steam railroad a hundred years ago, and now again we see transportation conditions entirely revolutionized by the development of the automobile, attended by a tremendous expansion of improved highways, requiring numberless wide, permanent bridges.

Indeed, many observers see a complete revolution in our social life as a result of the universal use of the automobile, a new era of decentralized homes and factories, depending upon good roads and good bridges for quick and safe transportation.

The key to our newest civilization seems to be the improved highway; may it be made not only commodious and permanent, but beautiful as well—especially the bridges that carry it over streams and other obstructions, and constitute its most monumental features.

That this result may be accomplished, may

we not look forward to much closer cooperation than now exists between the engineers and the architects?

In earlier days it was possible for one person to acquire the artistic training and scientific knowledge needed to perform the functions of both architect and engineer. This was accomplished by Sir Christofer Wren and by Jean Rodolphe Perronet.

In their time the preparation required for these professions was comparatively simple, but modern conditions demand far more training and experience than can be expected from an individual.

Collaboration between architects and engineers is, therefore, necessary, and should begin with the inception of the work.

It is evident that when the general design of a bridge is left solely to an engineer whose training has been entirely along scientific lines, and then an architect is called in consultation, the latter must necessarily confine his work to decorative treatment. On the other hand, when the general design of a bridge is entirely in the hands of an architect who, perhaps, has had inadequate scientific experience, the engineer is limited to the thankless task of giving sufficient strength to the structure, the general conception of which violates the rules of scientific design.

The best interests of bridge architecture can be served in the future through the close cooperation of architect and engineer.

APPENDIX "A"

BIBLIOGRAPHY

OF PRINCIPAL WORKS ON BRIDGE ARCHITECTURE

Gauthier—Treatise on Bridges—Paris 1728.

Geo. Semple—A treatise on Building in Water—Dublin 1776.

Thomas Pope—A treatise on Bridge Architecture—New York 1811.

E. Gauthey—Traite' de la Construction des Ponts—Paris 1816.

Hann and Hosking—Theory, Practice and Architecture of Bridges—London 1842.

John Weale—Bridges—London 1843.

Smiles—Lives of the Engineers—London 1861.

Jeaffreson and Pole—The Life of Robert Stevenson—London 1864.

E. Degrand—Ponts en Maconnerie—Paris.

M. Paul Séjourné—Grandes Voutes—Paris 1913.

W. Shaw Sparrow—A Book of Bridges—London 1914.

George C. Mehrtens—A Hundred Years of German Bridge Building—Berlin 1900.

William Emerson and Georges Gromort—Old Bridges of France—1925.

Encyclopedia Britannica—Eleventh edition—1911.

The Builder—London.

The Engineering News Record—New York.

Engineering—London.

The American Architect—New York.

The Architectural Record—New York.

The Architectural Forum—New York.

APPENDIX "B"

GLOSSARY OF TECHNICAL AND ARCHITECTURAL TERMS USED

(Based upon Webster)

ABUTMENT   (of a bridge) The support at either end of the entire bridge.

AGGREGATE   (of concrete) The particles (of stone, gravel, etc.) which are united by the cement.

AQUEDUCT   A structure for conveying water over a river or hollow, more specifically called an aqueduct bridge.

ARCADE   A series of arches with the columns or piers which support them.

ARCH   A structural member, usually curved and made up of separate wedge-shaped voussoirs, with their joints at right angles to the curve. Scientifically, the arch is a means of spanning an opening by resolving vertical pressure into horizontal or diagonal thrust.

ARCH RIB   Used to designate a free standing arch having a width much less than that of the bridge, usually in pairs, and supporting columns.

ARCH RING   The arch proper, used to designate the arch without the spandrels, fill or other elements, and applied to arches which are the full width of the bridge.

ARTICULATED   Put together with joints, as a truss.

BALUSTRADE   A row of balusters (vertical supports) topped by a rail, serving as an open parapet.

BASCULE   (bridge) A counterpoised or balanced drawbridge, opening in a vertical plane.

BASKET HANDLED ARCH   An arch formed in the shape of a basket handle, may be either three or five centered.

BATTLEMENT   A parapet consisting of alternate solid and open spaces, surmounting the walls of ancient fortified buildings.

BEAM   A structural member, usually straight, supported at each end.

BENT   A frame put together on the ground and then raised to a vertical position. Also used to designate the vertical supports of steel bridges when assembled in place.

CANTILEVER   A projecting member; in a bridge, either of the two beams or trusses projecting from piers towards each other, their far ends free, or connected with a joining member.

CARTOUCHE   A tablet for ornament, usually for receiving an inscription.

CENTERING   The temporary substructure which supports the permanent construction.

COPING   The highest or covering course of a wall, used in bridge work to designate the finishing course of the spandrel walls.

CORBEL   A projection from the face of a wall, supporting a superincumbent weight.

CORNE-DE-VACHE   (cow's horn) Used to describe the practice of splaying out the ends of an arch by gradually increasing the span.

CORNICE   The horizontal member which crowns a composition; may consist of several courses of masonry.

CROWN   (of an arch) The vertex, or top part of an arch or arched surface.

CULVERT   A small opening or waterway under a highway, railroad, etc.

CUTWATER   The sharpened end of a pier, built with an angle or edge to better resist the action of water, ice, etc.

DENTIL   A small rectangular block in a series projecting like teeth, as under the corona of a cornice.

ENTABLATURE   The architecturally treated wall resting upon the capitals of the columns and supporting the pediment or roof plate.

EXTRADOS   The exterior curve of an arch; the exterior surface of an arch ring.

FASCES   A bundle of rods, having among them an ax with the blade projecting, borne before Roman magistrates as a badge of authority.

GABLI   The vertical, triangular portion of the end of a building.

GIRDER   An iron or steel beam of economical section, either made in a single piece or built up of plates, angle bars, etc.

GRILLAGE   A framework of sleepers and cross beams of timber or steel, used in foundation work.

HEADER   A masonry unit laid with its greatest dimension at right angles to the face of the wall.

INTRADOS   The interior curve of an arch; the inner surfaces of the arch ring.

KEYSTONE — The voussoir at the center of the crown of an arch, which, being the last to be placed, is regarded as binding the whole together.

LINTEL — A horizontal member spanning an opening, used to support superimposed loads.

MEDALLION — A shape resembling a large medal, as a circular, oval, or sometimes square tablet or panel bearing a figure or figures represented in relief, a portrait or an ornament of such a form, as a sculptured decorative architectural member or feature.

PARAPET — A low wall or similar barrier, as a railing, especially one to protect the edge of a platform, or a bridge, etc.

PEPERINO — A dark colored volcanic conglomerate, much used for buildings and bridges in Rome.

PIER — A support for either end of a bridge span.

PILASTER — An upright architectural member, rectangular in plan, structurally a pier but architecturally treated as a column with base, shaft and capital.

PILE — A large stake or pointed timber, driven in the earth, used to support piers and abutments and sometimes used as a direct support for superstructures.

PONTOON — A flat bottomed boat, or any float, used in building bridges, the boats usually connected with beams.

PORTAL — In bridge building, the space at either end, between the first two principal trusses in a truss bridge or a door, gate or entrance, especially one that is grand and imposing.

PYLON — A gate way building having a truncated pyramidal form.

QUAY — A solid artificial landing place, usually of masonry, at the side of a river, etc.

QUOINS — The selected pieces of material by which the corner is marked; in stone the quoins consist of blocks larger than those used in the rest of the building and cut to dimension.

RELIEVING ARCHES — An arch used to relieve another member, as a lintel, of part of its load.

RETICULATION — Masonry work constructed, or faced, with diamond-shaped stones, or square stones placed diagonally.

RISE — (of an arch) The vertical ascent of the intrados curve.

SADDLES — Blocks over which the cables of a suspension bridge pass, or to which they are anchored.

SCAFFOLDING — A supporting framework for temporary supports, usually of timber.

SEGMENTAL — An arch of which the intrados forms the segment of a circle, meeting the jambs or imposts at an angle.

SKEWBACK — The course of masonry, the stone, or the plate, having an inclined face against which the voussoirs of an arch abut.

SPAN — The spread or extent of an arch between abutments or of a beam, girder, truss, roof, bridge, or the like, between supports; also, the portion thus extended.

SPANDREL — The irregular triangular space between the extradox curve of an arch and the enclosing right angle; or the space between the extradoses of two contiguous arches and a horizontal line above them.

STRAIN — The deformation, or distortion, of a body due to stress or force.

STRESS — The force with which a body resists external forces.

STRETCHER — A masonry unit laid with its greatest dimension parallel with the wall.

TRESTLE — A braced framework of timber, piles or steelwork, for carrying a road, railroad, etc., over a depression.

TRUSS — An assemblage of members such as beams, bars, rods and the like, so combined as to form a rigid framework; that is, one that cannot be deformed by the application of external force without deformation of one or more of its members.

TUFA — A porous rock formed as a deposit from springs or streams, as travertine.

VOISSOUR — Any of the tapering or wedge-shaped pieces of which an arch is composed.

APPENDIX "C"

BIOGRAPHIES

IN the early history of modern bridge architecture, three great British engineers have taken a prominent part. These men are John Rennie, Thomas Telford and Robert Stephenson. The first is best known as a bridge engineer, the second as a highway engineer and the third as a railroad engineer; but they all designed great monumental bridges which marked distinct advances in the development of the art.

JOHN RENNIE

John Rennie, the architect of three great London bridges, including the New London Bridge, and many other engineering structures, was born at Phantassie, Scotland, on June 7, 1761. His father was a small farmer, as his ancestors had been for generations. Young Rennie was well educated, completing his studies at the University of Edinburgh in 1783, and immediately started upon his professional career, designing canals, docks and bridges, at which occupation he spent the rest of his life, allowing himself but little pleasure and having but limited interests outside of his own work. His death occurred in 1821 and he was buried in Westminster Abbey, near the tomb of Sir Christofer Wren.

THOMAS TELFORD

Thomas Telford, the designer of the Menai Straits Suspension Bridge, was also Scotch, having been born at Eskdale, Scotland, in 1757. His father was a shepherd and the son was brought up in poverty, learning the trade of a stone mason, at which he labored for many years, educating himself by reading in his spare time. This self-educated man had a great love for poetry and music. Much of his verse is in print. While the greater part of Telford's life was spent in building bridges and harbors, he is best known for the type of paved roads which he built and which are still known as Telford roads, the principle being that of the macadam road with selected sizes of stone for the various courses, large stone for the first course and progressively smaller for the upper courses. Telford was active in the formation of the Institute of Civil Engineers, was elected its first president in 1820 and left it a legacy upon his death in 1834. This self-educated son of a Scotch shepherd, who became a gentleman of wide culture, the friend and loved companion of poets and writers, is buried in Westminster Abbey.

ROBERT STEPHENSON

Robert Stephenson was born in 1803, the only son of George Stephenson, famous as the inventor of the railroad locomotive. Robert was educated at private schools and at the University of Edinburgh. While the father's greatest achievements were in the development of the railroad engine, Robert's principal work was in the construction of the great bridges required to carry the railroads over wide rivers. His best known work is the Britannia Bridge. He died in 1859 and was laid at rest in Westminster Abbey, near the tomb of Thomas Telford.

JEAN RODOLPHE PERRONET

Jean Rodolphe Perronet, the pioneer French bridge engineer, son of a Swiss soldier in the service of France, was born at Surennes, near Paris, October 8, 1708. At the age of six, Perronet was taken to visit the Tuilleries. The young Prince Louis XV, for whom elaborate amusements had been arranged in the adjoining gardens, was attracted by Jean and invited him to join his games. This was the beginning of a friendship which made Perronet the recipient of many unusual personal favors and confidences.

Perronet intended to enter the Genie Militaire, a military engineering school, but since only three candidates were admitted at a time, and these selected by promotion, he changed to the study of architecture.

In 1725, M. Debeausire, a Parisian architect, employed Perronet as assistant in charge of highway and sewer construction. In 1745, he was appointed administrator and inspector of roads and bridges for the district about Alencon. Two years later M. Trudaine Sr. founded a school of engineering in Paris, of which Perronet was made Inspector General and Director. About this time,

M. Hupeau, Chief Engineer of Roads and Bridges of France, entrusted to Perronet many of his duties. Meanwhile Perronet's reputation as an instructor in mathematics, physics and architecture made his services valuable as a consulting civil engineer. The Nogent-sur-Seine, the Sainte-Maxence, the Concorde at Paris and the Nemours bridges, also the Bourgogne and Yvette canals are among his achievements.

By order of the Council of State, Perronet was named Inspector General of the Salt Mines of France in 1757, which office he held until 1786. As an engineer, Perronet displayed unusual skill as a designer and administrator. His personal qualities of kindness, patriotism, amiability and arduous devotion to his profession won him the esteem of the London Society of Arts.

The last years of Perronet's life were devoted to a compilation of lengthy memoirs. He died at the age of eighty-six, February 27, 1794.

GENERAL TEXT INDEX

Note: The various bridges described are indexed by location.
See list of illustrations for index to plates.